95 Mistakes Job Seekers Make
. . . And How to Avoid Them

Books by Richard Fein

95 Mistakes Job Seekers Make...And How to Avoid Them

101 Dynamite Questions to Ask at Your Job Interview

101 Hiring Mistakes Employers Make and How to Avoid Them

101 Quick Tips for a Dynamite Resume

111 Dynamite Ways to Ace Your Job Interview

Cover Letters, Cover Letters, Cover Letters

First Job

95 Mistakes
Job Seekers Make

... AND HOW TO AVOID THEM

Richard Fein

IMPACT PUBLICATIONS
Manassas Park, Virginia

ISBN: 1-57023-198-2

Library of Congress: 2003100523

Publisher: For information on Impact Publications, including current and forthcoming publications, authors, press kits, online bookstore, and submission requirements, visit our website: www.impactpublications.com.

Publicity/Rights: For information on publicity, author interviews, and subsidiary rights, contact the Media Relations Department: Tel. 703-361-7300, Fax 703-335-9486, or email: info@impactpublications.com.

Sales/Distribution: All bookstore sales are handled through Impact's trade distributor: National Book Network, 15200 NBN Way, Blue Ridge Summit, PA 17214, Tel. 1-800-462-6420. All other sales and distribution inquiries should be directed to the publisher: Sales Department, IMPACT PUBLICATIONS, 9104 Manassas Drive, Suite N, Manassas Park, VA 20111-5211, Tel. 703-361-7300, Fax 703-335-9486, or email: info@impactpublications.com.

Contents

Dedication

In Honor of my Mother, Celia Fein, and my brother, David

Acknowledgments

95 Mistakes Job Seekers Make...and How to Avoid Them is my eighth book on career and employment issues. If you are looking for a job, or preparing yourself for a job search in the future, I think that you will find it very helpful in a practical and easy to use way. There are many people I would like to thank for their assistance. My publisher, Ron Krannich, and my editor, Mardie Younglof, have been of inestimable assistance throughout this project. Thanks also to my colleagues, Janis Dagilus, Kim Jones, and Carrie Carpenter, who bring sunshine with them every day at work. Theresa Arndt, Doug Cooney, Ted Daywalt, Robert Greenberg, Anne Hirsh and her staff, Glenn Kaufman, Lorraine Mixon-Page, Susan Oxford, and Dr. Ralph Shedletsky made special contributions for which I am very grateful. To my wife, Rhonda, and our daughters, my love forever, even when I am not writing a book.

Richard Fein
March 2003

95 Mistakes Job Seekers Make . . . And How to Avoid Them

1

Motivation Mistakes

YOU PROBABLY CHOSE THIS BOOK BECAUSE YOU ARE hoping to find a better job than the one you currently have or acquire new employment after being laid off, fired, or retired. While you most likely have the skills necessary for that next job, you may have difficulties landing the job because of mistakes you make in conducting your job search.

Based on numerous interviews with employers, this book identifies common mistakes made by job seekers. It's designed to help you avoid such mistakes so that you can go on to quickly land a job and advance your career. If you avoid these key mistakes as well as follow our advice for conducting an effective job search, you should be able to land a job you want.

This first chapter focuses on several mistakes that relate to your motivation. Taken together, these mistakes affect your attitude, personality, focus, energy, enthusiasm, and drive—important ingredients in any job search. Whatever you do, make sure your job search is based upon positive motivations. Otherwise, you will be less attractive to employers and more likely to jump from one unsatisfying job to another.

MISTAKE #1

Lack a clear, positive reason for changing jobs.

The first question to ask yourself is this, "Is the change designed to meet a positive objective I have, or am I simply trying to get away from where I am?" Stated another way, are you moving forward or merely fleeing? If you are simply fleeing, you may be going from one sub-optimal situation to another. Further, people who are simply seeking any job are actually less attractive to most employers.

Solution

Ideally, you want a new job for positive reasons—to help you achieve your goals rather than merely to escape from a negative job situation. Start identifying positive goals by making a list of professional and personal goals you hope to achieve. Some common goals might include:

- Better pay

- Greater opportunity for advancement

- More (or perhaps less) challenging job responsibilities

- Less (or more) business travel

- Better balance between your job and the rest of your life

Write down the three most important goals that you hope to achieve in your next job:

1._____

2._____

3._____

It is very important to have clear, positive motivations for seeking a new job. Avoiding negative reasons is no less important, as seen in Mistakes #2-6, below.

MISTAKE #2

Jump from the frying pan into another frying pan.

Your mindset is a critical part of your job search. The story of Sharon and Suzanne, who had very similar jobs working for the same company, provides a good case in point. Sharon was intent on leaving her current job. "I just can't stand this place any more," she said to herself. Suzanne had a different perspective. "I would be happier in a place that offered a significant challenge and the potential for advancement," she thought. What is the significance of this difference in mindset? Sharon is hurting herself twice over. First, she will be less attractive to other employers, for whom being enthusiastic about their company is a plus but simply being disgruntled is a negative. Second, if Sharon is offered a new job, she is more likely to accept a position that isn't a good fit. After all, her goal is simply to flee rather than to move forward. Suzanne, on the other hand, is more likely to search out jobs that potentially meet her positive goals and will interview better because her mindset is consistent with what an employer is seeking. Therefore she is more likely to be offered a job she would want and less likely to accept a job just for the sake of a change.

Solution

Consider changing jobs if you are strongly attracted to a new situation, not simply because of dissatisfaction with your current job.

MISTAKE #3

Let envy motivate you.

It is a mistake to let envy of others become the reason for seeking a new job. Envy simply causes dissatisfaction with your current job and displaces rational planning in the search for a new one. Yet some people decide to look for a new job simply because they believe that others have it better. Looking on the surface of things, somebody may appear to be better off in some aspect of things, let's say salary or office space. However, that does not mean that s/he is better off in all respects, that s/he is happier in any respect, or that you would be happier in his place. Would you sell your house and buy your neighbor's simply because his grass looks greener than yours?

Solution

Don't let envy become your motive for seeking a new job. The old adage, "The grass is always greener on the other side of the fence," contains some instructive lessons:

- Your neighbor still has to mow it. Along with the greener grass, your neighbor has the task of mowing it. Are you willing to pay that price?

- The grass isn't really all that green. Once you are on the other side of the fence and live with the grass every day, it may not appear all that green. Job changers often experience a bit of a letdown when their fantasized greener pasture turns out to be covered with as much manure as their previous place of employment.

- It's OK to admire your neighbor's grass, but the important thing is to value your own. Let's assume that your neighbor's grass really is greener and that maintaining it really isn't all that difficult. So what! Maybe grass isn't really all that important to you. What you should focus on is what makes you happier, not what your "neighbor" appears to have.

MISTAKE #4

Believe someone has a "perfect job" for you.

Wouldn't it be great to land the perfect job? It would certainly seem so. However, the standard of "perfect" can really get in your way. There are several reasons:

- Perfect today may not be perfect tomorrow. Companies change, jobs change and people change. Therefore the very notion of "perfect" isn't set in stone.

- There will always be days you would rather forget. On any job, some days are perfectly dreadful, totally frustrating, difficult to get through.

- "Perfect," even if possible, would depend on you. "That job would be just perfect for me," Ann thought. When she actually got the job, Ann realized that making the job "perfect" depended more on what she put into the job every day than the intrinsic responsibilities of the job itself.

- Finding "perfect" comes at a high cost. Harry passed on a significant number of good opportunities to continue his pursuit of "perfect." They required a huge amount of time in terms of both hours and calendar days. In the end, Harry had to accept a job offer just to stay afloat financially. Ironically, Harry started this potentially good job with a bad attitude. He felt he had settled for the job he took, rather than succeeding in his pursuit of that perfect job. That bad attitude made it hard for him to do well in his relationships with the other employees and to master the responsibilities he had accepted.

Solution

What you should really be looking for is a job that is a good fit for your skills, abilities and values—one that has the potential to bring you a great deal of satisfaction now and for the foreseeable future.

MISTAKE #5

Deja vu all over again.

Some people think that they *are* what they *do*. If they think, for example, that they are a teacher, that is the kind of job they will seek. A far better approach would be to say, "What I want in a job is (fill in several blanks), and therefore I will look for a job that potentially offers what I am seeking." Yes, you must be realistic. If you haven't trained as a doctor, you will never be a brain surgeon. But there are millions of jobs that need *skill sets* rather than *specific degrees* or *certifications*." Although looking for a job similar to your current one is likely to yield more interviews, what have you gained besides a paycheck if you aren't happy? When you are going for what you *want*, you will approach the job search with greater creativity and energy.

Solution

Remember, you are living in a free country with a multi-trillion-dollar economy. There are many opportunities that may be a good match with your skills, personality characteristics, and interests. Don't limit your job search to situations that are similar to your current position.

MISTAKE #6

Look for anything but the same job.

Just as damaging as restricting yourself to the same job in another place is its destructive opposite, looking for *anything but* the same job. In either case you are restricting your options based solely on what you have done in the past. It is more constructive to think in terms of *what you want next* rather than fleeing from anything that reminds you of what you have now.

Solution

Identify the specific things that make you unhappy about your current job. Is it the work hours, the length of the daily commute, your degree of autonomy? Try not to oversimplify the matter by saying to yourself, "I just can't stand this place." If the dissatisfactions that you want to leave behind are specific, you will have more latitude is seeking alternatives.

MISTAKE #7

Think that a job search is like instant coffee.

One important attribute for a successful job search is patience. That does not mean sitting and waiting for things to happen. Patience means the ability to take steps in the right direction with the understanding that it may be a while before things come to fruition.

Solution

This book recommends that you allow six months of serious effort for landing your next job. Obviously, the actual time needed will vary case by case, and the less robust the economy, the more time you are likely to need. Allowing enough time enables you to plan and execute your job search campaign without putting undue strain on your family or your current job. Your job search schedule might look something like this if you are currently employed:

- **First week:** Compile a list of positive reasons for seeking a new job.

- **Second week:** Identify any downside or risk associated with your job.

- **Third week:** Build an inventory of your strengths (job-specific skills, transferable skills, and personal attributes) and accomplishments.

- **Fourth week:** Establish your priorities for your new job. If two desired goals come into conflict, which priority takes precedence?

- **Fifth week:** Make a chart listing people (and their contact information) who might be considered part of your job-seeking network.

- **Sixth week:** Identify potential employers you want to contact. Start contacting people in your network.

- **Seventh week:** Write a new resume. That's right, a new one, and not just an updated version. Of course, after you have written a new resume, look at your old one for additional ideas.

- **Eighth week:** Draft a thoughtful cover letter. Start scouting for recruiting open houses and job fairs.

> **HINT:** Thorough preparation during the first eight weeks will make the following steps easier and more productive.

- **Ninth week:** Start applying for potential new jobs.

- **Tenth week:** Follow up on the previous week's applications. Apply for some additional opportunities.

- **Eleventh week:** Assess the responses (or lack thereof) to date. If you have been invited to an interview, focus on preparing for that. However, apply for at least one more job, so that you will always feel that you have another iron in the fire. Applying to *several* more jobs makes even more sense.

- **Twelfth week:** Your time now should be spent mostly on finding opportunities and pursing them. Over the next three months the seeds you are sowing will either sprout or turn up fallow. If it is the latter outcome, you should reassess both your goals and the approach you have been taking to achieve them.

You may be saying to yourself that 12 weeks is only half of six months. That's right! You will need time to prepare yourself for a successful job search and to get started. Once you are underway, it is only a matter of time. It is not unreasonable to anticipate an additional three months of outreach, interviews, follow-up interviews, job offers, and assessing or negotiating your offers. Then there may be a few weeks between accepting a new job and the actual start date. It is better to be prepared for a six-month effort and not need that much time than to need the full six months but not be prepared for that length of time.

MISTAKE #8

Lack sufficient financial resources for a six-month job search.

At some point you may need to seek a new job involuntarily. Unfortunately, this may happen because of adverse conditions affecting your current employer, or, even worse, affecting the entire economy. Part of being prepared for this possibility is to have financial resources sufficient to support you and your family for about six months. That is a reasonable period to allow for a job search, especially when it starts under duress. Having adequate financial resources means you will be more appealing to employers because you will be less emotionally distraught. Also, you will be less likely to accept a new job based solely on desperation.

Solution

To prepare for six months of financial resources, there are two obvious but often-neglected steps to take:

1. Develop a contingency budget you can live with if the need arises.
2. Save with rigorous regularity until you reach the amount of savings you will need.

Unfortunately, if you do find yourself involuntarily out of work, you may be especially vulnerable to the following mistakes.

MISTAKE #9

Take a check instead of a job.

Nancy has just lost her job in a downsizing. In her state, she will be eligible for unemployment compensation for 26 weeks if she continues looking for work but doesn't find a new job. At first, this seems like a no-brainer. Money for not working has a certain appeal and having open-ended time to look for a new job would seem to make the task logistically easier, especially in light of the hard work involved in looking for a job as noted above. However, life is seldom that simple.

    The risks for Nancy are that she will have too much unstructured time, will get out of the habit of working, and will raise doubts in the mind of a prospective new employer because she has been out of work too long.

Solution

To begin with, Nancy has to realize that this is not a no-brainer. Seemingly free money can come with an opportunity cost attached.

Nancy should ask herself these questions about a temporary job:

■ Would it help buttress my self-respect?

■ Is it possible that I will make connections that I probably wouldn't make otherwise?

- Would it be an opportunity to try a field or an industry that may have potential for the future?

- Could the temporary job grow into a regular job? (We tend to say "regular" rather than "permanent" these days in light of unfortunate reality.)

- Would a temporary job help avoid time gaps on my resume?

- Would it do more to organize my day than to take away available job search time?

If Nancy's answer is "yes" to at least one of these questions, the benefits of the temporary job may outweigh the seeming benefits of "free" unemployment compensation money.

2

Get Started on the Right Foot

MISTAKE #10

Fail to conduct a *smart* job search while keeping your current job.

David was looking forward to moving on to a new job and felt optimistic about his chances. After all, he had several job interviews already scheduled and was confident that at least one of them would result in a job offer. Unfortunately, he hadn't fully followed common sense in the process:

1. David hadn't given any thought about whether to inform his immediate boss about his job-seeking efforts. Many managers will not hold it against you if you tell them you are looking for a new job. They will, however, get quite upset if they hear about it from someone else, or if they suspect it based on your on-the-job demeanor. During his annual performance review two years ago, David's boss had said, "If I can ever help you, in this company or elsewhere in the industry, please let me know." David liked and trusted his boss, but still kept his job-seeking plans to himself. David should have weighed the relative risks of telling his boss rather than just ignoring the possible implications.

2. David did not keep control of where his resume might show up. That is, he applied for a nice-sounding job through a post office box number. The

recipient turned out to be a friend of David's boss. "If I wasn't going to tell my boss, I should have at least been careful about who else knew that I was looking," David reflected after the fact.

3. David neglected to perform his current job responsibilities to the best of his abilities while searching for a new opportunity. His mental energy went into a job he didn't have, and the job he already had began to suffer.

Any one of these three mistakes could have been sufficient to lessen David's job security. In fact, the combination led to his being among the first to be let go when his company downsized. Ironically, being out of work made David less attractive to potential new employers.

Solution

If you are confident that it is safe to let your manager know that you are considering moving on, do it. Otherwise, if you don't know whose hands your resume will fall into, it is better not to send it. Do not respond to box number help-wanted advertisements. If you are working with an executive recruiter (see Chapter 5), make sure that the ground rules preclude your resume being sent to anyone without your specific, prior approval.

MISTAKE #11

Leave in spirit before you have left in fact.

Patrick had been looking for a new position and had finally found it. "Now I can look forward to my new job and stop busting my hump around here," he thought. Patrick was on the verge of making a big mistake. First, people at his current company would remember Patrick's last weeks on this job more vividly than his initial weeks, and perhaps more than those in between. By slackening off, he was damaging his own reputation, something that would continue to have a bearing on his career until he retired. Second, Patrick was acting with questionable ethics. Since he was still on the company payroll, his current employer had every right to expect that Patrick would continue his best efforts until his last day.

Solution

Remind yourself of this as often as necessary: Ethical considerations and your own self-interest both mandate that you continue to work at a high professional level right through your final day at your current job.

MISTAKE #12

Leave in anger.

Dahlia had been very unhappy on her job at Thenco, in large measure because she felt that her boss was unfair and that her co-workers never really made her feel welcomed. She landed a job at Newcompany after a three-month search. On her last day at Thenco, Dahlia exploded in anger, giving vent to every hostile feeling she had long stifled for fear of losing her job. Despite the fact that she had made some positive contributions to Thenco, her outbursts on the final day became the clearest memory anyone had of her. When she subsequently sought another new job, she wasn't able to get a positive reference from Thenco, a significant barrier in her career development.

Solution

If you need to express anger, do it at a time and place that won't cost you professionally. Trusted family and friends might be good listeners and will hopefully keep what you say to themselves. You might also want to consider a competent professional such as a clergyman or a psychotherapist. Blowing up on the premises of the place of employment you are leaving or bad-mouthing a former employer to another employer are not acceptable options.

MISTAKE #13

Fail to deal with negative emotions when you lose your job.

Dr. Ralph Shedletsky is a partner at GSW Consultants, a leading human resource consulting group with offices and affiliates in North America and abroad. As a consultant and career coach with years of experience, he advises clients who are leaving a job involuntarily. Often these people are burdened with emotions that get in the way of finding the right next job, as understandable as those emotions may be.

Solution

Emotions you should be aware of include loss of trust, loss of self-esteem, and fear of the unknown.

TRUST. Many people feel a loss of trust, perhaps even a sense of betrayal when they are laid off or fired. For example, when Patrick lost his job, he felt that his expectations about his relationship to his employer had been violated. What did Patrick do?

First, he examined his expectations. He had held an unspoken assumption that the company—or more personally, his immediate boss—had entered into a kind of fiduciary relationship with him. That is, he felt that in return for his best efforts on the job, his job would be protected. In reality, the company had a fiduciary relationship to its stockholders, and Patrick's boss was responsible to the company. No one had an obligation to protect Patrick. When he came to understand what the obligations of others to him actually were, his feeling of betrayal was much diminished. Second, Patrick clarified in his own mind who had "done him wrong." Was it his specific boss or, more broadly, the company? Deciding that it was his boss, Patrick spoke with her about the business reasons for his dismissal. "The issues involved were much bigger than you as an individual or me as your boss," she replied.

It was to Patrick's benefit that he did not globalize from his immediate experience to the world of employment in its entirety. If he had felt that all managers are untrustworthy or that all companies are unfair, he would have been operating under needless burdens as a job seeker. His sense of distrust would impair his ability to succeed at a job interview. If he had taken a new job before he came to terms with his sense of betrayal, he would likely have brought a poisonous attitude with him that would have made his new job situation difficult and even perilous.

SELF ESTEEM. Many people identify intensely with their job, and losing it makes them feel less of a person. A job search is more painful to people with wounded self-esteem, because every rejection (and they are almost inevitable) strikes them more profoundly. Further, their interviews are liable to suffer if they are perceived as a person suffering esteem problems rather than as one who is confident in his/her abilities. A common result of esteem problems, if not addressed, is that you are more likely to accept a job that just isn't right for you simply to end the agony of job search rejection.

Loss of self-esteem is understandable, but all out of proportion to reality. Stand back a moment and view your situation in a larger perspective. Don't judge your life by a single event. Instead, think about your achievements and accomplishments in that job and in your broader life. In fact, make a point of writing down these successes in some detail. That way your thoughts will tend to coalesce around your competencies instead of your recent setback.

FEAR OF THE UNKNOWN. Don has just been told that his job has been eliminated. "Yesterday, I knew what I was doing and who I am. Today, I don't know either," he thought. Fear may paralyze him, but he must move forward. One thing he can do, as he plans for his future, is to focus on achieving things about which he is passionate. When Don begins planning for a future that is more to his liking, his anxiety will tend to recede and may even be replaced by excitement. Of course, after Don has planned for his passions, he needs to take objective reality into account. Seldom does anyone achieve everything that s/he wants in a job. Still, Don can now proceed with a job search motivated by his goals instead of his fears.

FINANCIAL ANXIETY. Along with job loss comes a loss of income. While you may receive a severance package and/or unemployment insurance, you will still need to have other resources available. Preparing a financial cushion in advance, before you lose a job, will alleviate your anxiety.

MISTAKE #14

Believe that looking for a job is just like having a job.

Many people say that looking for a job is a full-time job in itself. Life would be easier if that were actually true. Unfortunately, the need to find a new job may consume more than the proverbial 40 hours a week. While having a job means we perform our tasks within some framework of expectations, being out of work is more like being your own boss (except that you are not deriving income). It can be an open-ended activity with no obvious limit. Therefore, you may need to work "overtime" to achieve your goal. This can be disconcerting. "I am working harder for no pay than I did when I had a job," you might think.

Solution

First, realize that for the next three to six months the task of finding a good job may require many hours of work, evenings, and weekends included. Second, at the same time, you need to find a balance between job seeking and the rest of your life. Put aside time to be with your friends and family. Find some activities that give you a break psychologically when you are not pursuing that next job physically.

MISTAKE #15

Fall prey to discouragement.

For most people, receiving "no interest" letters is far more common than being invited to an interview, and it is easy to become discouraged. Here are some ideas for maintaining your morale throughout your job search.

Solution

Maintain your morale through your job search by:

- **Continuing to add irons to the fire:** Applying for new jobs should be part of your weekly routine. Knowing that your resume is being reviewed by five to ten additional employers every week helps maintain morale and lessens your anxiety about any one specific employment situation.

- **Pursuing informational interviews:** They tend to be easier to arrange and keep you actively involved with people in the field. Informational interviews can also generate job leads.

- **Being realistic**: A good resume will open interview doors, but maybe not on your first or second try. You are likely to hear "no" more often than "yes." But you will get to "yes," and you only need one job at a time.

MISTAKE #16

Become complacent.

When Barry asked what Larry was doing with his job search, Larry said, "I have two interviews scheduled for the end of the month." Barry was glad for Larry, but asked, "What are you doing between now and then?" Larry answered that he was preparing for his forthcoming interviews (a vital effort in itself) but that he had stopped applying for other jobs.

Solution

Having interviews on your schedule is no reason to stop searching for additional opportunities. After all, an interview is not a job offer, and you may not want to accept the job even if it is offered. Besides, knowing that you are creating more options will help you face with less anxiety the interviews you have scheduled.

Let's take complacency one step further. Your resume has earned an interview for a wonderful job. Your interview goes well, the job is offered, and you accept it. Now picture the scene: The curtain goes up on your first day of work. Do not expect to hear applause from your employer. On the contrary, your audience will be expecting a great performance. Winning the job is a chance to do the job. Applause will come when you have done the job well. Don't become complacent once you have the job in hand!

3

Research

MISTAKE #17

Not know how to identify potential employers

Shirley has written a great resume and has drafted a good cover letter that she can mold to meet individual situations. If she doesn't know how to identify potential employers, these documents will be all dressed up but have nowhere to go.

Solution

There are a multitude of sources to identify potential employers:

1. **Use online job search websites**

   Numerous websites post job opportunities online. One of the most complete directories of such sites is AIRS: www.airsdirectory.com/jobboards. For starters, try these popular sites:

   www.ajb.dni.us
   www.employmentguide.com
   www.flipdog.com
   www.joboptions.com
   www.monster.com

   www.careerbuilder.com
   www.federaljobsearch.com
   www.hotjobs.com
   www.jobtrak.com
   www.thingamajob.com

2. **Use a search engine (even when you are clueless)**

   When you don't have a particular website to check out, or want to explore sites other than those listed above, use a search engine such as Google, Ask Jeeves, AltaVista, Lycos, MSN, HotBot, and others.

3. **Explore links to other websites**

   One benefit of using a search engine is uncovering links to other sources which may be of interest to you. For example, let's take a hypothetical company and call it Flashco, a maker of flashing lights for railroad crossings. The same screen that identifies Flashco may identify URLs for related topics such as Flashco's competitors, railroads and major manufacturers of lights.

4. **Check a prospective employer's website**

   Many companies, including small ones, have a website. It is a convenient way to present potential customers and investors with important information about the company. In many cases, they also post employment opportunities. Once you have connected to a company's website, look for a link that says something like "Employment Opportunities" or "Careers at [name of company]" and double-click. Determine if you are interested in any of the opportunities indicated, and if so, note how the company suggests you respond. If conventional mail is called for, your paper resume, accompanied by a cover letter, is appropriate. If an email resume is preferred, see MISTAKE #51 on page 52.

5. **Continue to utilize conventional sources**

   Remember that computer resources are not the only tool to use. Conventional, non-computer sources are still valuable. Let's look at a few of them.

   > **Chambers of Commerce:** Most communities have a local chamber of commerce that fosters business interests in that area. A chamber is a great place to obtain a list of local employers. Often such a list even indicates size and industry of the employer. Thus, a microbiologist could ferret out the names of potential employers by seeking companies that might be doing work in microbiology. Another individual might use the list to prod his/her thinking about a potential industry to enter.

   > **Local press:** The local press often carries stories about businesses in the area, such as new, expanding, or significant companies, or the top 100 companies in some category. A useful approach is to send your resume to a person mentioned in the

press article. Your accompanying cover letter should make immediate reference to the article. For example:

1776 Heritage Drive
Jenkintown, PA 19075

March 25, 2004

Mr. Harry Fine
Director of Marketing
Incongruous Products, Inc.
1643 Central Ave.
Havertown, PA 19067

Dear Mr. Fine:

The story in today's Havertown Herald about Incongruous Products, Inc. was really impressive. I was especially struck by your statement that growth in the sale of ice cubes to Arctic Circle residents has been phenomenal.

My own professional experience includes marketing products to seemingly incongruous customers. For example, I established an outlet for snow shovels in Key West, Florida, and a mail order business in beef patties for vegetarians. The annual revenue is $1.5 million and $24 million respectively.

Perhaps we could discuss a marketing role for me at Incongruous Products, Inc. My resume is enclosed. I will call you next week to see when a meeting can be arranged.

Sincerely,

Celia Ginzi-Bird

Celia Ginzi-Bird
Enclosure

Note: The details of this letter (e.g. ice cubes, snow shovels, beef patties) are obviously intended to add a light moment to your reading of this chapter. The actual examples in your letter would not be as improbable as these are.

6. Standard references

Standard references may be helpful in identifying potential employers. Examples include:

> *The Million Dollar Directory (Standard & Poors)*
> *Hoover's Handbook of American Business (Hoovers)*

Your reference librarian can help you find additional books that are held in your local library.

MISTAKE #18

Ignore small companies.

Smart fishermen go where the fish are. Yet many people overlook small companies, even though that's where the jobs are. According to the Small Business Administration, companies with fewer than 500 employees employ about 55 million workers. As a subset of that, companies with fewer than 100 employers employ about 40 million people. Using either measure, small businesses account for about half of the total employment in the United States. Yet many people ignore these businesses or hold them in disdain.

Solution

Become familiar with the potential disadvantages and advantages offered by small companies, so that you can access that job market better.

Potential disadvantages include:

- **Lack of name recognition.** Small companies may not have a high profile, especially outside of their local area. Therefore, you may be less likely to search out their website or recognize their name from an Internet job board. Small companies may require more effort to find. On the other hand, they are likely to attract fewer job applicants with whom you will be competing.

- **Lack of diversity.** Many small businesses appear to have a lack of demographic diversity. However, that may reflect their geography rather than an anti-minority or anti-female culture. Don't assume that a company is a less desirable place to work simply because only a few of the group with which you identify strongly are presently found among the employees. In fact, you may want to be the trailblazer for others in your affinity group to follow.

■ **Inadequate fringe benefits.** There is a common perception that smaller companies are less generous with fringe benefits. If you are interested in a job opportunity offered by a small business, you can examine the fringe benefits as a legitimate but separate issue.

Potential advantages offered by small businesses:

■ **Concern about their employees.** Smaller companies often care more about their employees as people, in part because the managers and/or owners are apt to see them daily and even live in the same community.

■ **Variety and impact of responsibilities.** Of necessity, smaller companies are likely to offer the opportunity for broader, more varied tasks that may have a greater impact on the company. That can make your workweek more enjoyable and provide a training ground for future professional development, as you add to your career skills.

■ **On-the-job training.** Larger companies are often viewed as providing better training, but that is not necessarily so. Hands-on, on-the-job training may be less sophisticated than classroom-style training, but it is more appealing and efficacious for some people. Also, those who plan to start their own business down the road often find working for a small business first is a great training ground.

MISTAKE #19

Ignore employment prospects that are perceived as "unglamorous."

John wanted a job with lots of glamour. America is a free country and everyone is entitled to his/her own sense of values. However, through his preoccupation with "glamour," he was shortchanging himself by ruling out of consideration the majority of employers in the United States.

Solution

Understand the reality of "glamorous" workplaces in order to avoid ignoring prospective employers and missing out on a rewarding career.

■ First, there are thousands of companies and nonprofit organizations in America, but only a relative handful would be regarded glamorous by anyone.

■ Second, what is glamorous when viewed from the outside may lose its shine when experienced by working there every day.

- Third, glamorous companies are not necessarily profitable companies. Everyone knows about the dot.com wreckage strewn across corporate America in the late '90s.

- Fourth, John is setting himself up for a rude awakening. When people look for a glamorous employer, they are often hoping that their place of employment will impress others. By seeking status associated with being in the employ of a "glamorous" company, John is vulnerable to the indifference or even hostility of others to his employer's name.

MISTAKE #20

Respond incorrectly to a job ad.

Responding incorrectly to a job ad can reduce your chances of getting invited to an interview.

Solution

It is important that you respond to a "Help Wanted" ad exactly as requested (with one exception). For example, note whether you should submit your resume by hard copy, fax, or email, and proceed accordingly. If an email is requested, send your resume in the body of your email unless you are requested to submit an attachment. In all cases, your cover letter should include in the first paragraph a reference to where you saw the notice and the applicable job title or number.

On some occasions, you may be requested to call a particular individual. The company may want to see if you have the ability to call a stranger, a tool that is especially useful in sales. You should be prepared for a telephone interview on the spot. You may be asked to call a certain telephone number with no name attached. When you do so, don't be surprised if the response invites you to work through the company's Interactive Voice Response (IVR) system.

We mentioned one exception above. The ad may ask for your salary history or salary requirements. Do not fall into this trap. Respond with a general statement such as," Salary requirements are reasonable and competitive with the field."

MISTAKE #21

Approach job fairs incorrectly.

If you don't seek out job fairs, you are overlooking a way of connecting with companies and organizations under one roof. Job fairs are a great way to meet with company representatives face to face. It is your opportunity to be the person be-hind the resume, which is also a benefit to the company. Meeting 100 real job seekers is more productive than reading 500 resumes submitted by faceless people. There is also an advantage to you in that companies may be represented at the fair that might not have been on your outreach radar screen otherwise. In the business section of newspapers, in trade journals and on the Internet you can find informa-tion about career fairs that may be of interest to you.

Solution

You can maximize your benefit from a job fair by following these recommendations, which have worked for many participants at job fairs.

Go. The investment of a small amount of your time can yield a significant number of useful contacts. However, if you need to keep your job search secret from your present employer, you may not want to pursue job fairs.

Dress appropriately. You will look and feel more professional if you wear business attire. In general, a suit and tie for men and a suit or pantsuit for women will help you create a positive first impression.

Introduce yourself properly. For example, greet the company representative with a firm handshake. Say something like, "Hello, my name is John Greene. I would like to learn more about career opportunities with your company." If true, you could add, "I am especially interested in _____ op-portunities," and/or, "I am familiar with your company from my current job (or "From reading your website after I found out that you would be at the job fair today").

Communicate. Don't just drop off your resume. Talk with the company represen-tative. Have some good questions ready, such as:

1. To what extent are skills like teamwork and communication important to your company?

2. What responsibilities would a new hire have?

3. What would a typical week be like for a new hire?

4. How would you describe the working environment in your company?

5. What qualities are you looking for in new (engineers, accountants, teach-ers, etc.)?

6. What are the best/worst aspects about a job with your company?

7. What personal attributes are necessary to succeed in (your profession, your company, this position)?

8. Why did you choose to work at this company?

9. What is the average length of time an employee remains at your company?

Business card. Ask for a business card. Sometimes you may not get one, but you lose nothing by asking, and you get an instant record of whom you spoke with at the fair.

Follow up. After the fair, follow up with each company of interest to you. First, write a brief letter like the one below. Your letter can be either emailed or sent by hard copy. Second, call about one week later. You will probably get an answering machine. That is all right. Your letter and subsequent call will increase the possibility of your getting a job interview because, by following up, you have demonstrated a degree of interest, professionalism, and perseverance.

SAMPLE FOLLOW-UP LETTER AFTER A JOB FAIR

October 4, 2004

Ms. Jean Jones
Associate Analyst
ABC Corporation
1234 Main Street
Philadelphia, PA 19152

Dear Ms. Jones: [Note: if Gabrielle is sending an email, she would start here.]

It was a pleasure meeting with you at the Middle Management Mavens Job Fair held in the Sheraton Hotel on October 3. I enjoyed our discussion about career opportunities for financial analysts at ABC Corporation.

I am interested in pursuing the possibility of a position with ABC. For your convenience I have enclosed another copy of my resume. [If sending an email say, "For your convenience, I have included another copy of my resume below."]

Next week, I will call you to discuss what our next step should be.

Sincerely yours,

Gabrielle Chan

Gabrielle Chan

4

Networking

MISTAKE #22

Neglect to achieve name recognition in your field.

Imagine yourself as a person who is well known and well respected in your field. Wouldn't that make your job search easier? Of course it would. Consider these advantages:

- **Networking.** When you reach out to people in the field whom you don't know personally, it is more likely that they will agree to help you because people love to connect with those having an established reputation. Besides, people with recognized names are more likely to be viewed as acquaintances than as strangers.

- **Headhunters.** Executive recruiters are more likely to find you because your name will surface when they do a keyword search on Google or another large search engine.

- **Referral to hiring managers.** Corporate human resource professionals will feel more confident showing your resume to a hiring manager if you are perceived as something of a known or at least credible entity.

Solution

So how do you establish your reputation? You don't need a Harvard MBA or to appear on a TV financial news program. Speak at professional events, such as trade association conventions, or write articles for professional and trade publications. The Internet is all about content, so websites are always looking for articles to keep their readers coming back. The fastest way to get your name out on the Internet is to get involved in discussion forums. Discussion forums are easy to participate in and many organizations have them. Check them daily and share your wisdom and knowledge. Before you know it, you'll be known as a respected source to audiences relevant to your professional interests. Your name will start to surface in Internet searches and some people in your field will know of you from personal experience. For job-seeking purposes, you become something of a known entity instead of a completely unfamiliar name.

MISTAKE #23

Network inappropriately.

In job-seeking terms, a network is that group of people who may be willing to help you in your job search for personal, professional, or purely altruistic reasons. The people in your network are those who can give you advice, insights, and perhaps leads to specific job opportunities. There are several mistakes job seekers make when networking:

- Avoid approaching friends and family because of a misplaced sense of embarrassment or not wanting to mix personal and professional aspects of life. People like to help other people. Besides, someday you may be able to return the favor. The rich and the powerful aren't embarrassed to ask for help. Why should you be?

- Neglect building a professional network before they need it.

- Fail to relate well to people in their network.

Solution

- **Define your personal network broadly.** Your network should include not only friends, family, and neighbors, but also family of friends and friends of family, etc. In terms of your personal network, include not only your nuclear family but also aunts, uncles, cousins, nieces, nephews, in-laws, and step-relations. In fact, you may also include people outside of your family with whom you have a close relationship, such as your pastor, physician, attorney, accountant, or financial advisor.

- **Build your professional network before you have need of it.** That means building positive relationships with everyone you meet through your job and retaining their contact information where you can get to it. Your professional network could include present and past co-workers, members of trade and professional associations, customers, and even friendly competitors. Obviously, do not put anyone in an awkward position or compromise professional relationships. Also, do favors for people before you ever have to ask anything from them.

■ **When you need job-seeking help, ask for advice, not an interview.** When you conduct an informational interview, be mindful of the other person's time and obligations; thank him or her and keep him posted as your search progresses (it's easy to do with email).

CAVEAT: Only approach those whom you trust to hold your job search in confidence. If not sure, don't ask. Remind each person of the sensitive nature of your inquiry and ask, "May I tell you something in the strictest confidence?"

Let's take a look at how Lauren built her network. She had been out of the workforce for a number of years, so she didn't have any direct connections in the field she was exploring—the mutual fund industry. She identified three categories of people who could be helpful:

■ **Warm calls:** Family members, friends, and neighbors, all of whom would be glad to hear from her.

■ **Tepid calls:** Friends of family members, neighbors of friends, and other individuals whose names were given to her by people on her "warm calls" list.

■ **Cold calls:** People in the industry who were complete strangers.

Lauren approached her warm calls and asked each person if they had friends, neighbors, family members, or professional associates in the mutual fund industry. One neighbor's tennis partner was a broker-dealer named George who often advised clients about mutual funds. The neighbor asked George if Lauren could contact him, and he agreed.

Lauren's questions to George helped her learn a great deal about mutual funds from a broker-dealer and client perspective. "I have gained practical insights I wouldn't pick up from a newspaper or a book," Lauren realized. She also asked George if he could suggest a few names of people in mutual fund companies whom she might contact. Lauren assured him that she would pursue informational meetings with those individuals, and not ask for a job. George was so impressed by Lauren's preparation and professional demeanor that he agreed. "In fact," he told her, "Sally Forth at Mutual Money mentioned over lunch that she was looking for a good client communication person. Why don't you contact Sally and be sure to mention my name?"

Receiving more than she had asked for, Lauren mailed Sally a cover letter and resume right away. At the same time, she sent a brief note to the other names (Ishwar and Janice) George had supplied. Because she was seeking **information** from these two individuals, Lauren did not include a resume. As it turned out, she succeeded very quickly in arranging an informational meeting with Janice, who gave Lauren a deeper understanding of mutual funds. By the time, she had a formal job interview with Sally two weeks later, Lauren had enough information to present herself as a competent individual who understood client communication and the demands of the mutual fund industry.

Another job seeker, David, was interested in other ways of identifying prospects for information interviews. "For example, I am considering mall management, but I don't know anybody in that field," he said.

Rhonda, a friend, suggested that David explore his local mall. "I bet they have a manager's office right there. Why not inquire about the manager's name and title, then request a meeting?" David sent a brief letter before calling the manager with his request:

1776 Heritage Drive
Philadelphia, PA 19102

May 10, 2004

Mr. Vernon Rapp
Director of Mall Resources
Albion Property Management
76 Bells Corner
Philadelphia, PA 19152

Dear Mr. Rapp:

I am in the process of exploring a change in career. Mall management is a field I have identified and I would appreciate your insights and suggestions about the pragmatic issues involved with this career. Could you spend 15-20 minutes with me to discuss this industry?

Let me give you some personal background. For nine years I have worked in transportation logistics. Although I remain well employed, I am seeking other avenues for my talents. A recent article in *Retail Management* magazine attracted my interest in mall management as a possible next step.

Your time is precious and I promise to respect it. I will call you next week in the hope that you can offer me the benefit of your advice.

Sincerely,
David Goodman
David Goodman

MISTAKE #24

Fail to take advantage of a corporate alumni association as part of networking.

An alumni association is typically thought of as a group of people who graduated from the same high school or college, but today there is a growing phenomenon of *corporate* alumni associations. This type of association is formed by former employees of a company who wish to preserve relationships they have established for personal, social, or career reasons. Unfortunately, many people are unaware of this great source of leads and support.

Solution

Glenn Kaufman, founder and president of Corporate Alumni, Inc. (corporatealumni.com), is an expert on the subject and points out these mistakes that job seekers might make:

A. If your current or former employer has a corporate alumni association, it is a mistake to:

    Ignore its online directory. All the alumni associations that my organization helps to establish have an extensive online directory. Members tell about their present employers, their current projects, what they have been doing for the last five or ten years, and even their hobbies. When you find somebody of interest (perhaps someone you once knew, but not necessarily) you can request an informational conversation with him or her through a "form and forward" message system. This is an excellent way to expand your professional network. Also, it is a great source of ideas. Often people read another alum's directory information and think, "Hey, I never thought of that. If s/he left here and is doing that type of work, maybe I could too."

    Not know about association job boards. Many corporate alumni associations have job boards. A person at New Company may post a position that he or she has become aware of or even a position that reports directly to him or her. In those cases, you have a "friend in court" in addition to uncovering a job that you may never have been aware of otherwise.

    Neglect the "members' news" section. A great way to keep fellow alumni aware of the exciting things you are doing is to submit material about your current job to the Members' News section. When people are thinking about hiring a new person, the Members' News provides a source of updated professional information.

    Fail to become active. Joining the Steering Committee, sponsoring a reunion and similar activities give you a higher profile and help you make deposits in the "alumni favor bank."

B.   If your current company and past employers do not have an alumni association, it is a mistake to:

Not find a friend who can give you access to one. You may be able to gain access to an association through a friend who is a member. Since many alumni associations include current employees, they may be a source as well. Also some associations have guest log-ins. It pays to find out.

Not know how to find an association. There are three main sources: Corporate Alumni, Inc. website, the specific company's website, and a good search engine such as Google.

Not start your own corporate alumni association. It is easy, inexpensive, not time consuming, and may even be sponsored by the parent corporation. Sponsoring a reunion of some old friends may be a simple, innocuous way to start.

Assume associations are rife with negativity. In fact, negative gossip is very rare. Members want to convey and participate in positive interaction.

5

Executive Search Firms

Doug Cooney, President of Deerfield Associates Executive Search, Inc., a retained executive search firm, points out a number of mistakes that job seekers often make when using an executive search firm.

MISTAKE #25

Think that the search firm will automatically be interested in working with you.

This mistake often results from not differentiating between **retained** and **contingency** search firms.

Solution

Understand the difference between retained search firms and contingency search firms. Companies hire a **retained** firm to conduct a search for positions they need to fill. The retained firm thus starts with a specific search and is most interested in a job seeker who might meet the needs of their specific client. Typically, a retained firm handles searches for positions with a salary of $100,000 or more. A **contingency** firm starts from the other direction, receiving a fee if and when the firm makes a placement in a client company. A contingency firm tends to handle positions carrying a salary of less than $100,000. Its recruiters look for job seekers with a profile that they may be able to match with a potential client who might be looking for that particular professional profile.

MISTAKE #26

Fail to ask about the executive search firm's specialty.

Most executive search firms have a specialty—for example, financial services. No matter how talented the firm is, they probably can't be of much service if your area of interest is in another field. You should be aware that since executive search firms are generally hired by their clients to fill specific skill sets, career changers might have a challenge getting the recruiter's attention.

Solution

Be sure you deal with a firm that specializes in your field.

MISTAKE #27

Respond poorly when an executive recruiter contacts you.

Not all firms are the same, and you need to know with whom you are dealing if you sign on with them.

Solution

If an executive recruiter contacts you, *listen* to what s/he has to say, and *ask* if they are retained or contingency. Before agreeing to work with that recruiter, meet in person and make sure that you like and trust them. If time or distance precludes a face-to-face meeting, at least ask for references from recent people whom the recruiter has helped. Research the firm's website and check it out in *Kennedy's Directory of Executive Recruiters* before agreeing to work with that firm. At the same time, remember that playing hard to get is a counter-productive strategy. Being open and cooperative is a good way to start off, even if you ultimately decide not to work with the recruiter.

MISTAKE #28

Lose control of your resume.

Not being aware of where the resume may end up could cause problems for you with your current employer, if they don't know you are searching for another job.

Solution

You are well advised to ask the search firm to refer your resume to clients only after consulting with you. This minimizes potential conflicts with your own search, having an overly aggressive recruiter send your resume to huge numbers of employers, and the possibility that your resume could end up on your boss's desk. This is generally important only with contingency firms. Don't give your resume to a recruiter whom you don't know or haven't met.

MISTAKE #29

Assume the search firm will work with any job seeker.

The executive search firm is not your butler taking your laundry to the dry cleaner. Much to the contrary, the search firm has to use its time well and must decide which job seekers are worth taking the time.

Solution

When you contact a firm, you should send a solid cover letter delineating your selling points along with a professional resume. Mentioning in your cover letter who referred you to the search firm is also good idea.

You can send your cover letter and resume via email and then follow up by telephone a week later. One advantage of email, Doug Cooney notes, is that it is an easier modality for responding to you, even if the message is simply to recommend another firm that is more likely to be helpful to you.

MISTAKE #30

Think the executive search firm will find you a job.

A good search firm will do what they can to *connect* you with good interviews. Be sure you ask the recruiter for their advice and input relative to their client/your possible future employer. Once you get an interview, the rest is up to you.

Solution

Don't neglect your own networking and outreach efforts. Ask the firm if they object to your pursuing connections with other search firms. Retained firms are more likely to feel comfortable with that since they have defined clients and therefore other search firms wouldn't be referring you to the same companies for interviews.

MISTAKE #31

Take advantage of the firm's contacts on your own.

After Myrna was told that the firm was trying to arrange an interview for her with a large bank, she contacted the line manager at the bank on her own. It is both unethical and unwise to do that. Myrna abused her relationship with the search firm and also blew the interview opportunity. Why? The bank lost interest in a person who didn't behave in a straightforward manner from the very beginning of the potential relationship, and the recruiter lost interest in this candidate for future searches.

Solution

Deal with the firm in an honest and straightforward way, keeping your dealings above board.

MISTAKE #32

Forget to follow up after the interview.

Getting an interview through the services of an executive recruiter doesn't mean overlooking follow-up afterward.

Solution

You should still send a thank you letter to your interviewer(s) after the interview. It is important that you also contact your executive recruiter and let him/her know what transpired. "Don't make your executive recruiter chase after you," Doug Cooney advises. "That could lose you an important ally in your job search."

6

Before Putting Yourself on Paper

MISTAKE #33

Lack an inventory of your positive characteristics.

Before you even write a resume, you need an inventory of your positive characteristics. Without it you will lack many of the building blocks you will need for a successful resume and material to draw upon during a job interview. Also, you will be missing out on a list of nice things about yourself that you can review whenever the job search gets discouraging and your morale starts to sag.

Solution

Compile an inventory of positive characteristics describing yourself. Broadly speaking, there are three types of inventories you can build. In fact, many people develop all three inventories.

1. **Your own positive characteristics:** To develop this list, you need to examine thoroughly your work experiences and activities to identify the positive skills and attributes that you possess.

2. **Generic characteristics:** Some characteristics are important across many fields. An inventory of generic skills you possess will help you with your resume, cover letter, and interviews. Examples include leadership, conflict resolution, problem solving, honesty (especially in an awkward situation), teamwork,

sound decision making, dealing with change, giving and receiving criticism, time management, communication (written and oral), persuasiveness, handling pressure, initiative, dealing with difficult or unpleasant situations.

3. **Specific characteristics needed by a prospective employer:** An alternate approach is to identify the specific characteristics needed by the prospective employer to whom you are directing the resume, then match those which you have with their needs.

Starting with your own positive characteristics has the advantage of being more inclusive. This is an especially good approach if self-reflection is one goal for writing your resume. A generic inventory helps you identify characteristics that are important but which you may overlook because you assume "everyone" has that skill. Starting with the employer's specific needs quickly focuses on selling points you need to highlight. It is particularly useful for those who are already clear about their professional goals and/or want to develop a new resume in fairly short order.

Let's take a closer look at each of the three types of inventories.

1. **Your Own Positive Characteristics: A "Start With Yourself" Inventory**

    David was an experienced professional who wanted to switch to a new field. Before taking such a major step in his life, he needed to conduct a self examination. He wanted to identify as many of his positive characteristics as possible. To do this, he turned to various sources.

    Job Description: David reviewed the job description for his current position. He noted that a credit analyst at his bank "analyzes data submitted by individuals and businesses seeking loans; determines credit worthiness and degree of associated risk; advises loan committee on appropriate action in documented report." Based on this part of his job description, David included analyze, determine risk, advise, document in his inventory.

    Performance Review: Since David's performance had been reviewed annually by his manager, he examined his most recent performance reviews for inventory ideas. His manager had referred to him as "diligent," "insightful," thorough," and "highly respected." David immediately added those characteristics to his inventory. He also noted that his manager was less enthusiastic about David's volume of output. This latter point wouldn't make a good resume item, but it did alert David to a topic he might have to address during a job interview.

    Work Diary: David started to keep a diary of his daily work life. His purpose was twofold: First, he wanted to capture positive characteristics not expressed in his job description or performance review. In writing his diary, David noted that he had to utilize a considerable degree of subjective judgment in his job since loan applicants' financial data really didn't provide everything he needed to consider. Second, David also noted in his diary what he enjoyed about his job and what he didn't. This information wouldn't provide a resume item, but it might help him identify new career alternatives.

Conversations With Colleagues: David listened to his colleagues. From the water cooler talk with other credit analysts, he realized that internal politics were an integral part of the job. "I would think more than twice before recommending against a loan request from a crucial client," one of his colleagues mentioned. David thought about this comment and put a positive spin on it: "Considers the larger goals of the organization" was added to his inventory.

2.   **Inventory of Generic Characteristics Many Employers Might Want**

Some characteristics would be appealing to most employers irrespective of the specific position that is to be filled. For example:

- Leadership

- Organizing

- Communication

- Problem-solving

- Hard-working

- Reliable

- Self-starting

- Intellectual curiosity

- Team player

The degree to which each of these characteristics is important will vary according to the situation, so simply loading these characteristics on your resume is probably not a good idea. Later we will explore stressing the most important characteristics for a specific resume goal.

3.   **Specific Characteristics Inventory**

There are characteristics which may be important in one job but far less important (or even undesirable) in another. Let's take a look at two job seekers considering specific characteristics for their respective next jobs.

Rhonda was a business professional seeking to move up in her current profession, marketing. She knew from experience that the ability to analyze marketing data was critical to her success. She also knew from discussions with peers that a healthy respect for budgetary constraints was essential. Successful people in her field were flexible, but decisive, a balance sometimes difficult to maintain. Rhonda wrote analyze, budget conscious, flexible, decisive in her specific inventory, knowing that she could add more characteristics later.

Gabrielle, a budding microbiologist, also started to develop her inventory of specific characteristics. A thorough knowledge of microscopic organisms and their characteristics and growth was clearly essential. Given Gabrielle's particular interest in Talking Horse Syndrome (THS), a knowledge of the relationship between organisms and disease, in addition to the effects of antibiotics on microorganisms, was quite important. Like Rhonda, Gabrielle needed analytical skills, albeit they would be applied to scientific, rather than marketing, data. Gabrielle began her inventory of specific characteristics with Knowledge of microorganisms, relationship between organisms and disease, and analytical.

If you are not well versed in the requirements of a specific type of job that may be of interest to you, here are two sources you can utilize with good results:

> **Informational Interviews:** One way to find out what it takes to do a specific job well is to ask people who have that job. A common name for this method is an informational interview. It is particularly appropriate for Larry, a college senior; Lauren, who is returning to the workforce; and David, who hopes to take the next step in his current career. Some people may find that less formal means of gathering information are more appropriate, such as business lunches, professional conferences, and observations of more senior managers.

> **Help Wanted Ads:** You can make good use of Help Wanted notices in building your specific characteristics inventory, since these ads usually contain a statement of skills and attributes the particular employer wants.

In the Mistake that follows, we will look at a necessary next step: Developing examples to validate the positive characteristics in your inventories.

MISTAKE #34

Lack Examples of Your Characteristics.

Your inventory of characteristics will not be very useful unless you take the next step and cite examples to support your characteristics. The examples may become building blocks for parts of your resume, lend credibility, and are likely to be vital if you are invited to an interview.

Solution

A good way to develop examples is to build a sentence for each characteristic, with the personal pronoun "I" being omitted. For example:

> Persuaded manager of another department to drop his objections to my marketing plan.

The chart below shows how you can develop examples of the characteristics you have listed. The wording in the chart is not in resume form since its purpose is to record ideas for your later use in a resume.

CHARACTERISTIC	SPECIFIC EXAMPLE
Hard-working	■ Worked an average of 60 hours per week to meet deadlines.
Organization	■ Organized annual meetings, including presentations, promotional literature, and conference logistics.
Communication	■ Wrote manual for new employees describing company philosophy, operating policies, rights and obligations. ■ Presented new product design to board of directors, utilizing PowerPoint visuals, detailed charts, and appropriate humor.
Analytical	■ Analyzed laboratory data to identify possible correlation between smog levels and traffic. ■ Analyzed census data to determine which demographic categories were best candidates for new deluxe edition of long- existing products.
Knowledge of microorganisms	■ Earned degree in microbiology from top-ranked university. ■ Researched impact of antibiotics on microorganisms while at Cellmate.
Flexibility	■ Demonstrated flexibility by incorporating interests of four departments into master marketing plan.

Decisive	■ Decided to pursue Tough Toenail product and development despite ambiguous data and conflicting departmental input.
Empathy	■ Empathized with employees concerned about job loss, but still instituted efficiency programs.
Initiative	■ Initiated research on alternative health care packages.
Persuasion	■ Persuaded management committee that displacing workers with machines would be very expensive in the long run.
	■ Persuaded reluctant staff member to try a new approach.
Integrity	■ Recognized for integrity by receiving "Employee of the Year" award.
	■ Accepted potentially unpleasant consequences from signing off on data which conflicted with the prevailing view.
Time Management	■ Completed all projects on or before schedule.
	■ Managed project involving contingent processes and uncertain lead times.
	■ Achieved excellent grades while working 30 hours a week.

MISTAKE #35

Confuse describing yourself with describing your job.

Should your resume describe you or describe your job? It would be a mistake to ignore the distinction or not to plan your resume based on your own circumstances.

Solution

If you want your next job to be closely related to your present or most recent job, focus your resume on those aspects which the positions have in common. On the other hand, if you are changing careers you should focus on your skills and at-tributes. Forthcoming college graduates are, in a sense, career changers, as they move from college life to the workplace.

Joan is a business-to-business sales manager looking for a less onerous travel schedule. Her resume will focus on her achievements in her current job, such as increases in market share and the development of her sales force. Judy, on the other hand, is a school administrator seeking to go into business-to-business sales. She will highlight her time management, communication, and interpersonal skills. In addition, Judy will make a point of showing that she understands the meaning of financial issues as a motivator and a resource, perhaps through her well thought-out decisions on school budget issues.

MISTAKE #36

Not know what sections should be included on your resume.

Composing a resume can be a daunting task, but not knowing its main compo-nents can make resume writing even more difficult.

Solution

Become thoroughly familiar with the components of a resume in order to facilitate the development of your own.

1. **Heading:** Provides your name and contact information, including street address, telephone number(s), and an e-mail address. Every resume must contain this contact information.

2. **Summary (or Objective):** A short statement starting with skills and at-tributes you possess that would be important for your next employer and ending with a succinct but informative statement about the kind of job you are seeking. The summary is very important if you are changing ca-reers or just leaving college, but not critical if you are looking for a posi-tion very similar to your current job.

3. **Experience:** This section presents your most directly applicable positive characteristics, usually in the context of some job you have had. This section should show the employer that you have already demonstrated the very attributes and skills that they need.

4. **Education:** At a minimum, list your college degrees and the conferring institutions, highest and/or most recent degree first. If you are a forth-

coming or recent college graduate, this section should probably come before Experience and may be used to show any number of positive characteristics through such rubrics as: leadership positions held, skills developed through research and group projects, the fact that you worked 20 hours or more per week to pay for educational expenses.

5. **Other Selling Points (OSPs):** Strengths you have that don't fit neatly as part of Experience or Education. Examples include computer skills, knowledge of languages, and civic awards. OSPs would typically go toward the bottom of your resume. However, use your judgment. If you are applying for a computer information systems position, it would make sense to have a complete section on computer skills located near the top of your resume.

MISTAKE #37

Fail to properly allocate resume space.

A resume must do much more than simply state facts. An employer will spend only a limited time reviewing a resume, with 30 seconds or less being the commonly accepted rule of thumb. Your resume must catch the employer's attention. Therefore, if you don't know how to utilize space to the maximum advantage, you lessen your chances of being invited to an interview.

The principles below are valid for both paper and electronic resumes, since human eyes must read even an electronic resume on a computer monitor or a printout.

Solution

Know and apply the following rule for utilizing space:

The more important a selling point is, the more prominent it should appear on the resume.

There are two ways to give a selling point prominance:

1) Put it early in your resume

2) Devote a lot of text to it

Therefore, the most important selling point on your resume should take up more space than any other single point, and it should come as early in the resume as possible.

David had held three substantive positions, and his current job contained the strongest selling points. Therefore, in his Experience section, he placed his current job first and allocated the most space to it.

EXPERIENCE

Current Company   Manager of Planning
            (Detailed description here)

Previous Company   Director of Forecasting
            (Brief description here)

First Company   Planning Analyst
            (Brief description here)

Jeannine was in a different situation. She was looking for a position in the technology industry and wanted to highlight her selling points from her technology experiences. However, for the last two years she had worked in financial services. Jeannine could organize her Experience section this way:

PROFESSIONAL EXPERIENCE

Technology Industry
    Gizmo Computer Storage Device, Bethesda, MD

Financial Services Industry
    Credit Commercial Bank, Fairfax, VA

MISTAKE #38

Assume an old resume can be recycled.

Writing a resume isn't all that much fun, and some people will simply update an existing resume when they begin a new job search. That is generally a mistake for several reasons:

- Your resume should be designed to entice a prospective new employer to interview you. Your existing resume probably didn't have that employer in mind.

- Your existing resume doesn't reflect ideas and insights gained from people in your network whom you have met since you wrote it.

- Your perception of yourself and your strengths may have shifted. At the very least, you should review your abilities and strengths to see how they have changed since you wrote your last resume.

Solution

Start anew, using the tips in this chapter and Chapter 7. Then go back to your old resume to determine if it contains anything compelling that isn't in your new resume yet.

MISTAKE #39

Use the same resume for all prospective employers.

Failing to customize your resume to various prospective employers can harm your chances of being invited for a job interview. Think of the ways that a product can be honestly advertised. A car may be presented for its speed and style to young singles and for its safety features to families. Similarly, your resume is not a fixed entity. It is perfectly ethical to modify what you present to various potential employers to reflect your strongest selling points for that situation. Unfortunately, job seekers won't make useful modifications for one of two reasons: 1) "I am the same person, why should I change my resume?" 2) It takes time and effort.

Solution

First, you are indeed the same person, but there are so many wonderful things you could say about yourself, you couldn't fit it all on one resume. Therefore, you need to be selective based on what is most important in any given circumstance. Second, if you have prepared your resume as suggested earlier, you will know your strengths and will simply need to reframe them to more directly address the interests of a specific employer.

MISTAKE #40

Forget that your resume reflects your value.

If you feel that writing your resume is a burden, a task that just needs to be completed, you are not likely to invest the time, energy, and creative thought that a good resume requires.

Solution

Remember that your resume is an investment in your career that will pay you back in five different ways:

1. **Self-analysis:** Since the subject of the resume is you, writing the resume well forces you to scrutinize your professional self.

2. **Inventory of your strengths and accomplishments:** Before you sit down to write your resume, you need to develop an inventory of your strengths and accomplishments so that you can present the most applicable of them to a potential employer in an easy-to-read and credible way. Even those items that do not ultimately appear on your resume can be useful in writing a cover letter or as a source of examples to cite at your job interviews.

3. **Identification of your weaknesses:** The characteristics that you cannot honestly include on your resume may be viewed as weaknesses by some employers. Therefore, you might try to find opportunities on your current job or elsewhere to demonstrate, achieve, or learn the characteristic you are missing. If you are invited to an interview, be prepared for questions about these possible weaknesses.

4. **Preparation for interviews:** The effort you put into writing your resume also helps you prepare for interviews. After all, if you are invited to an interview it will be because your resume shows a potential match between the job and your skills and accomplishments. Your interviewer will probe how and why you did what your resume indicates. Therefore, the thought that you put into writing your resume will help prepare you for many of the questions the interviewer is likely to ask.

5. **Establishment of the interview agenda:** Your resume will often serve as a source of interview questions. For example, if you wrote on your resume "reduced administrative expenses by 10%," your interviewer may be prompted to ask, "Tell me how you went about reducing administrative expenses." Therefore, what you write on your resume helps to set the interview agenda.

7

Resume Writing

MISTAKE #41

Make common resume mistakes.

Don't torpedo your chances by making the common but avoidable mistakes outlined below.

Solution

Become familiar with and avoid these classical mistakes:

Wrong focus: If you have a career objective stated on your resume, make sure that it is at least related to the job for which you are applying. For example, a marketing objective makes no sense on a resume sent to a company controller, who would be seeking to hire accountants.

Poor appearance: This includes illogical construction and sloppy use of space. If your most current job is closely related to your hoped-for next job, a chronological resume makes sense. A chronological resume presents your work experience in reverse chronological order—that is, the most recent experience comes first. If on the other hand, you are seeking to change fields, a category or functional resume would probably work better for you. A category resume organizes your experiences into job categories or functional skills, with the category most relevant for your next job coming first. In either event, devote the most space to the work experience that has the greatest relevance to the position you are applying for. You want to present yourself as a strong candidate for that job.

Misspelled words and poor grammar: Using the Spell-Check on your word processor is not enough. Both "manager" and "manger" will pass a spell-check, but you were probably never a mid-level "manger." Use a dictionary to double-check any word on which you wouldn't bet your mortgage. Also, read your resume from bottom up, in reverse order. This approach will help you read word by word, a good way to check poor spelling.

HINT: If you apply to a company having a number of locations nationwide or even worldwide, you should state in the Objective or Summary of your resume where you prefer to work. There is no need to be elaborate. Simply write, "Planning to settle in the _____ area" or "Willing to relocate as necessary."

MISTAKE #42

Start each resume "sentence" with a verb that doesn't convey your positives.

The first word of a resume "sentence" is the most important. It sets the tone for the entire sentence, identifies the point you are trying to make, and may be the only word the prospective employer reads.

Solution

You should start each "sentence" with a word that best represents the positive characteristic your prospective new employer needs. Verbs are usually the most appropriate for that purpose. For example:

"Wrote reports..." implies the ability to write.

"Researched databases..." implies that you have experience in research and with computers.

Some verbs do not indicate a positive characteristic needed for your next job. For example:

"Performed audits on a client to determine..." Not a bad thing to do, but are you trying to convey the characteristic of performing, as in singing or acting? It is better to get straight to your positive characteristic: "Audited clients to determine...."

Similarly, "Conducted survey...." Do you want to conduct an orchestra or conduct electricity? Probably not. Go straight for your positive characteristic, "Surveyed..."

MISTAKE #43

Misuse acronyms.

An acronym is a word formed from the initial letter of the words for which the letters stand. NATO (North Atlantic Treaty Organization) is an example. Most acronyms are not universally known, and you will not be communicating your message if you make a mistake in using them.

Solution

Here are two guidelines for the proper use of acronyms.

1. Use an acronym without further explanation if it is generally understood in the profession or company to which you are applying. For example, Rhonda might use PIMS on her resume without explaining that it stands for Profit Impact of Marketing Strategy if she plans to apply for another job in the marketing profession, since this acronym would be understood immediately by anyone in that field reading her resume.

2. On the other hand, using an acronym would not be useful if it is used only in a specific company or among a small group of people that doesn't include your next employer. Lauren uses a computer system known by people in-house as FLUKEY. No one outside her present company would have a clue as to what that acronym means. Therefore she should avoid the acronym entirely and say something like, "Reduced turnaround time by 10% by initiating new uses for company's existing computer system."

MISTAKE #44

Use meaningless words.

Some words are perfectly good in many situations, but shouldn't be on your resume.

Solution

Here are two examples of common useless words to avoid:

Assisted: Remember that your resume should tell your prospective employer about positive characteristics that you can bring to the job. What does "assisted" say about you? Perhaps you sharpened pencils or re-arranged the conference chairs. Think about what you demonstrated, achieved, or learned that was of value. Rather than write, "assisted in creation of new product," it is more informative to write, "Researched potential price points for new products" or "Identified market for gizmos, contributing to introduction of a new product line."

Responsible for: When you use this dry-as-dust language, you are sacrificing impact. Instead, you should use an appropriate action verb that conveys a positive characteristic. Compare "Responsible for accurate and timely filing of monthly reports" to "Filed accurate monthly reports, often beating deadlines." You can clearly see that "Responsible for" doesn't indicate how well you did the job or what you achieved. It doesn't belong on a lively resume.

On a related point, when you say something positive about yourself (e.g., researched, identified) you are not implying that you were the only person who did so. There is no need to write, "One of fifteen people who researched...." If you want to include teamwork or participation, write, "Identified untapped market for gizmos as part of a fifteen-person team."

MISTAKE #45

Overuse modifiers.

Modifiers (e.g., adjectives and adverbs) can be marvelous when writing an essay, but use them sparingly when writing a resume. The reason is that extra words often muffle impact instead of enhancing it.

Solution

Examine your resume for sentences containing adjectives and adverbs.

"Cooperated <u>closely</u> and <u>effectively</u> with engineering team to design marketable gizmo."

Eliminating the adverbs will result in a sentence with more impact:

"Cooperated with engineering team to design more marketable gizmo."

Modifiers in a resume context often add nothing to the significance of a sentence. After all, no one would write, "worked remotely and ineffectively"! The space you save by omitting modifiers helps you make your resume appear less crowded. Alternatively, you could use the space for a statement of greater value, such as results. For example, "Cooperated with engineers to design a marketable gizmo that increased revenue by 10%."

Adverbs are especially ill advised at the beginning of a sentence.

Adjectives, too, are often extraneous. For example, "Wrote <u>excellent</u> proposal…" Since no one would write, "<u>mediocre</u> proposal," the word excellent doesn't add anything.

MISTAKE #46

Use negative terminology.

Your resume will be more appealing if you use positive words and phrases. Resume language that is half full is more powerful than language that is half empty.

Solution

Here are some examples of negative and positive language. Avoid words that convey failure, problems, inadequacy, and other negatives.

Negative Terminology

- Avoided disaster
- Threatened underachievers
- Only 1/3 of projects failed
- Limited revenue loss to 20%
- Developed chemical compound that didn't explode

Positive Terminology

- Rescued
- Motivated staff
- Achieved 67% success rate
- Recognized 80% of original value
- Developed stable, non-exploding chemical compound

MISTAKE #47

Be too verbose.

When you use more words than necessary to convey a thought, you lose impact. "Less is more" is a good rule of thumb in resume writing.

Solution

Use one word instead of two where possible. Here are some examples:

Too verbose	More effective
In regards to	regarding
As well as	and
In the course of	when
From time to time	periodic (or periodically)
More than 50	50

MISTAKE #48

State over and over the same characteristics.

Jeannine has good analytical skills that would be important to her next employer. She would certainly want to have one or two resume sentences start with the word analyze when she writes about her current job in the Experience section. On the other hand, she does not want to make her resume seem redundant or one-dimensional by writing repeated sentences using analyze for her current job or by writing about her analytical skills in each of her previous jobs.

Solution

In general, each experience should be used to convey a positive characteristic that has not already been presented. Rhonda has done analytical work in each of her three jobs. In presenting her experience at her current employer, Rhonda articulated her analytical skills. Therefore, it is probably not necessary for her to repeat "analyzed" when writing about her experiences on her previous jobs. An exception would be a situation where analytical skills were the single important skill needed in the next position Rhonda wanted, or the nature of the analysis was significantly different on various jobs.

MISTAKE #49

Create doubt about your legal authorization to work.

Are you legally authorized to work in the United States for an unlimited period without restriction? If you are a U.S. citizen or Permanent Resident of the U.S., the answer is yes. If you are in the U.S. on a tourist visa or a student visa, or you are here illegally, the answer is no. If there is anything on your resume that might raise a doubt about your work authorization, you should clarify the matter.

Solution

A simple approach is to include a statement like this at the bottom of your resume:

Citizenship: Citizen of the U.S. (or Permanent Resident of the U.S.)

This clarification is an especially good idea if you have received a degree from a non-U.S. university, served in a foreign army, have no previous work experience in the U.S., or have a name that is associated with illegal immigration in your part of the U.S. While this last point is a sensitive one for many people, you should understand that even an employer with the best intentions in the world might make subconscious assumptions that could be a barrier to inviting you to an interview. Why not clarify the matter? In an age of terrorism and military conflict, well-intentioned, fair-minded employers may be reluctant to interview applicants who, they fear, are not legally authorized to work.

On a much smaller point, some people have taken on nicknames because their first name is hard to pronounce. They may put their nickname in parentheses after their proper name. Similarly, some first names are not clearly indicative of gender. In that case, you could indicate your name in the header of the resume as Mr. or Ms. (For example, Mr. Leslie Jones.)

MISTAKE #50

Fail to address possible objections.

Salespeople need to overcome objections that their prospective customers might have. Since a resume is a sales document, it should address and hopefully overcome some common reservations that an employer might have about an applicant in the following situations:

Situation	Solution
Returning to the workforce: The unstated objection might be that you are out of touch with your profession.	Show your current connection with your relevant work world through memberships in the appropriate professional organizations, your knowledge of technology currently in use (such as industry-specific computer packages), and the clear presentation of positive characteristics that are important to the job you are hoping to get.
Changing fields: The suspicion may be that you are a malcontent or that you have failed in your current job.	It is especially important to show your successes in your present field and any professional recognition you received (if any).
Recent college graduate: Because some young adults are unfocused and/or have unrealistic expectations, employers may fear you are that way also.	Show that you worked at least part time while in college (if at least 15-20 hours per week, show the specific number of hours worked). If you had a co-op or internship in a "real world" environment, make sure that fact is clearly visible. Your summary should mention not only important positive characteristics but also a clear career goal.

MISTAKE #51

Forget that the electronic age has changed some of the rules.

We have discussed the basics of avoiding mistakes in writing your resume. It is important to remember that there is often an electronic element involved in your job search, and this reality implies some important considerations. Susan Oxford is Director of Training and Development at AIRS (Advanced Internet Recruitment Strategies). AIRS conducts job search seminars that teach job seekers how to utilize the latest Web-based technologies to accelerate the job search process. AIRS is also a global leader in e-recruitment training. Susan's expertise will help you avoid a dangerous job-seeking mistake:

Solution

The electronic age has changed the corporate recruiting function from one driven by paper to one driven by electronics. This means that you will now be submitting your resume electronically instead of on paper. Further, your resume will probably be stored in an electronic database and accessed through an Applicant Tracking System (ATS).

Let's look at some practical implications. Your resume has to impress a machine before a human being will read it. Therefore, if you are submitting your resume by email, there are some pitfalls to avoid:

> **The subject line.** Don't get cute or fancy, because if you do, the recipient is more likely to trash your email than to read it. Instead, state the position and the location of interest to you, and the position number if you are responding to a notice.

> **Missing or inappropriate cover letter.** Your email should be more than merely a message of transmittal, but it will be a bit different than a traditional cover letter. After stating the position of interest to you, your next paragraph should say words to this effect: "As you will note from my resume, I have met all the requirements you have specified. In addition, I offer you the following…" (Caveat: Make sure that any accomplishments you mention are already publicly available information rather than proprietary.) You may also want to mention in the final paragraph that the resume included in the email "has been adapted to meet the needs of an Applicant Tracking System. A hardcopy resume or an email attachment will be sent at your request." The benefit of that statement is this: Once they have identified a candidate of interest to them, many headhunters or corporate human resources people will want to present a traditionally formatted, hardcopy resume to the applicable hiring manager.

> **Be careful of attachments.** Your resume should be included in the body of the email unless you have been specifically requested to send your resume as an attachment. The reason is that many recruiters will not open attachments from people whom they do not already know. Also, many companies will not open attachments because of security reasons.

> **Differences in resume format.** In addition, there will be some significant differences in resume format. The resume you send by email or submit to a job board on the Internet will be devoid of **bolding** and underlining. Instead, you will use CAPITAL letters to accentuate especially important words. In addition, you will use spacing and dashes as an organization tool and produce your resume in a bland typeface such as Times New Roman. Do not try to replicate the style of your

resume in an email. For example, you will want to keep everything left-justified. The purpose of all this is to minimize the degree to which your resume gets mangled as it transits from a word processor to email and from email to a database.

Retrieving your resume. Don't forget that you also want your resume to be retrieved. Since the recruiter will use a keyword search to find the resumes s/he wants to review, you need to write your resume with the keyword search in mind. One good way to do that is to have at least two (and perhaps four) specific sections of keywords. These sections should be at the very top of your electronic resume. In order to accommodate these keyword sections, a two-page resume is entirely acceptable.

- **Skills/characteristics.** In this section, write the words that describe positive characteristics that are important to the kind of job you want. For example: analytical, writing, teamwork, product management. For some positions you could list your computer skills or your technical expertise here.

- **Qualified for these job titles.** In this section you could list the job titles for which you think you are qualified. The reason for doing this is that the recruiter may search your resume utilizing a job title that is not identical with your current or past titles.

- **Location (or relocation).** List the major metropolitan areas to which you are willing to relocate. This is important if you currently live in Boston, for example, but the job is in San Diego, or if the willingness to relocate is a requirement of the job.

- **Certifications.** In some professions, certifications are important criteria. In those cases, explicitly listing your certifications may be the most important single part of your resume. They should be listed under your list of organizations.

MISTAKE #52

Forget to follow through after sending your resume.

A great resume and outreach plan are critical to your success in winning interviews, but there is also another step: follow-through. Omitting this step can cost you an interview opportunity.

Solution

Make a chart like the one below so you can track the outcome for each resume you submit.

Name of Company	Contact Person (Title)	Phone Number	Action to Date	Next Step
Wonderful, Inc.	Harry Stone (Director of Finance)	(413) 976-1881	(April 1) left message on machine	Call again on April 9
Fantastico	Celia Goodman (Treasurer)	(617) 549-1987	(April 1) told resume deferred to HR Department	Call HR on April 9 ask who might have my resume
Dry, Inc.	Ellen Wettly (President)	(508) 876-1396	March 31– E.W. out of town. Reads mail upon return on April 10	Short note to thank secretary. call E.W.
Hopeful & Hightime	Janice Dagi-Ellis (Finance Manager)	(413) 652-6521	Telephone interview scheduled for April 8 at 10:00 A.M.	Prepare for 30-60 minutes interview

One week after you mail a resume, call the individual to whom it was sent. You could say:

> "This is Doris Goodman. I am checking up on a resume I sent last week. I would like to make sure that you received it and whether you need any additional information from me. Can you tell me anything about my status?"

If you receive no informative response, call again a week to 10 days later. Your call is likely to be answered by a machine or a secretary who will simply take a message. That's all right. Calling can be a point in your favor. However, heed the warning below:

WARNING! Do not make a pest of yourself. Calling more frequently than every 7 to 10 days makes you a nuisance, not an interview candidate. If you receive a response that indicates that further inquiries are not welcome, say, "Thank you. I hope to hear from you when you have made a decision." If you are responding to a Help Wanted notice that specifies "no phone calls," honor that request.

8

Cover Letters

More often than not, your resume will be accompanied by a cover letter when you submit it to an employer. This would be the case whether you use the U.S. mail to send hardcopy text or utilize email, sending your resume as an attachment. Even when submitting your resume through an online template, there is usually an opportunity to include a cover letter. The most common exception to this practice is when you submit your resume to a prospective employer face to face at a job fair or open house.

MISTAKE #53

Misunderstand the value of a cover letter.

A good cover letter is an important part of your job search effort. It should add *value* to your resume rather than just repeating it. There are five ways a cover letter serves as a **value-adding partner** to your resume. You could use one or all of the following strategies, depending upon your individual situation:

1. *Highlight* items that are of particular importance to that specific employer, but which are not prominent on your resume.

2. *Reframe* items in a way that will connect them explicitly to the prospective employer's interests.

3. **Add new material** that is relevant to the specific job opportunity, but which isn't on your resume. Ideally, you would have re-written your resume to reflect this new material, but there may be occasions when you need to act quickly and don't have the time to revise your resume.

4. *Explain your interest* in that specific job and in that specific company. Typically, this will go in the third paragraph of your letter.

5. *Address "credibility gap" issues* that appear in your resume. If the employer looks at your resume alone and spots something that seems irregular, you may have a problem. For example, you live in New York but are applying for a job in North Dakota. In that case, you should explain your connection to North Dakota. Perhaps your fiancée or elderly parent lives there. Suppose you have not had work experience during the past six years because you were at home with a child, but are now ready to return to the full-time workforce; you should say so. Un-addressed credibility gaps diminish your chances of being invited to a job interview.

Sometimes it helps to understand a concept better through an example that combines your imagination with the contemporary art of applying for a new job. Many people are familiar with a biblical story of Noah and the Flood. Imagine for a moment that you are Noah and are interested in a position as an insurance underwriter. Your resume appears on page 59. The annotated cover letter below would be a good partner to your resume because it **highlights** and **reframes** important material in your resume. In addition, the cover letter explains your **motivation** for seeking that specific job and adds **something new** that wasn't on the resume. Even with a good cover letter like this one, no one can guarantee that Noah will be flooded with invitations to job interviews, but his prospects will certainly be much stronger.

Ararat Drive
Ancient City, World 10001

October 1, 2004

Ms. Leah Methuselah
Vice President - Underwriting
Woodcraft Insurance Company
1849 Golddust Boulevard
Burbank, CA 91510

Dear Ms. Methuselah:

I am interested in becoming an underwriter for Woodcraft Insurance Company. My work experience and education should make me an asset to your firm. For example:

Expertise in wood products: Built everything from household items to houses.[1]

Team work: Involved seven people in Ark Management tasks during the Great Flood.[2]

Analytical skills: Straight "A" student in analytical and quantitative subjects while earning a college degree.[3]

I am particularly attracted to Woodcraft Insurance for several reasons. [4] First, underwriting is a career which combines the analytical, and personal skills I enjoy applying. Second, Woodcraft insures products in which I have both a professional and avocational interest. Third, I am planning to settle in the Bay area after my wedding later this year.[5]

My resume is enclosed. I will call you next week to see when a meeting can be arranged at your convenience.

Sincerely,
Noah Arkman
Noah Arkman

Enc:

_____

(1) Example of highlighting
(2) Example of reframing
(3) Example of something new
(4) Example of explanation of interest
(5) Example of addressing credibility gap (e.g., in this case geography)

(Noah's Resume)

Noah Arkman
Ararat Drive
Ancient City, World 10001
(999) 666-5678
Email: markman@arco.ararat.com

SUMMMARY of Qualifications:
Proven skills in leadership, communication, and problem solving. Demonstrated ability to assess risk and respond appropriately. Professional experience with The Flood and Reconstruction. Seeks to build a career in insurance, with a special interest in flood insurance. Interest developed as result of leading role played in worst disaster in recorded history.

WORK EXPERIENCE:
Flood Beater, WORLD RESCUE, INC. 2002-Present
Led rescue of human and animal life from the Great Flood. Directed reestablishment of human life on earth. Assessed risk of destruction based on heavenly insight and gathering rain clouds. Responded by organizing thousands of creatures to board a custom-made ark in an orderly manner. Solved both logistic and staff problems while completing ark under tight deadline. Communicated directly with ark passengers, thus minimizing discord during forty rough days at sea. Learned how to manage massive enterprise with minimal resources.

Carpenter, NOAH'S NOTCH   1999-2002
Built structures ranging from bookshelves to family houses. Designed ark decks and accommodations for selected clients.

EDUCATION:
School of Hard Knocks
Bachelor of Biblical Administration
Major: Management
Honors: *"Righteous Man in His Generation"* awarded in recognition of high moral character and trust of contemporaries.

LEADERSHIP:
Chairman, Raven/Dove Contest
Vice President, Ararat 4-H

ACTIVITIES:
Rebuild after the Deluge Benevolent Society

MISTAKE #54

Neglect key components of an effective cover letter.

Your cover letter should be logically structured and business-like in tone. There should be four paragraphs:

First paragraph. Identify your purpose in writing. If someone known to the recipient suggested you write, state that fact clearly in the first sentence. It may be a good idea to include his/her title if that would help grab the recipient's attention. Identify the position about which you are writing. You could have a one-sentence summary of your qualifications, such as, "My *six years of applied experience in this field should make me an asset to your company*." (If true, you could also say something like this: "*I offer you everything your job description calls for, and more*.")

Second paragraph. Indicate the benefits you bring to the company, namely those qualifications the company needs which you have. Include a short example with each qualification. The style used in the Noah illustration above is easy to read and is also easy "to track" (i.e., to correlate the company's expressed *desiderata* with your qualifications). If you can offer even more than what the position requires, this is a good place to express it.

Third paragraph. State why you are interested in the specific job or type of job. Cite reasons why you want to work for that company specifically. You may also want to express an interest in the profession generally or the industry of which the company is a part. Your statements in this paragraph will indicate whether you have done your homework and if you are seriously interested in this particular opportunity. Be sincere, specific, and don't state anything as a fact if you are not certain that it is true.

Fourth paragraph. This is the place to mention your resume. Refer to your resume as "enclosed" in the case of hard copy. In an email, your resume will probably be "below," but it might be "attached" if the recipient has requested it that way. Make sure to state that it is **you** who will take the next step (i.e., you will contact the recipient the following week to see if a meeting can be arranged). An exception would be if you have strong reason to believe that the recipient doesn't want to be called on the telephone.

Each cover letter should be tailored to the *specific* job opportunity and company. All-purpose, generic cover letters that you could mass-produce and send to just anybody are generally not effective. If your letter is hard copy, it should be produced on high quality paper. Also, make sure to sign your letter in blue or black ink. Your letter should include your return address, the full name, title, and address of the recipient, and the date. Whether your letter is hard copy or electronic, make sure that there are no spelling or grammatical errors. Using Spell-Check is useful but not sufficient for this purpose. Use your eyeballs also. (Remember that *manger* and *manager* are both acceptable to an electronic spellchecker.) Use a dictionary if you have the slightest doubt about the proper spelling or usage of a word. If you are sending an email and have more than one account, use the one that utilizes your actual name rather than a moniker (e.g., Topguy123) that doesn't lend itself to name recognition and may appear to be unprofessional.

MISTAKE #55

Fail to address the employer's needs in response to a job ad.

Help Wanted ads, by whatever name, can be found on company websites, electronic job boards, and even in the more traditional print media such as newspapers and trade publications. In responding, whether by hard copy or electronically, your cover letter should address in a clear and easily visible way the characteristics the employer has indicated as desirable/necessary in prospective candidates.

Let's step outside of our day-to-day world again. Imagine that the biblical Joseph spots the following Help Wanted ad in a newspaper. This position would be a career step up from the prison into which he was tossed. He carefully reads what the potential employer (Pharaoh) wants in terms of skills and attributes from the person who will do this job, and crafts his cover letter accordingly.

HELPED WANTED

Seeking an interpreter of dreams. Must have a high sense of integrity, foresight. Education in the School of Hard Knocks highly desirable. Interested applicants should respond to:

The Senior Advisor, Pharaoh◻ Palace, Egypt.

Pit # 4
Prison
2000, B.C.E.

The Senior Advisor
Pharaoh's Palace
Egypt

Dear Mr. Senior Advisor: [That's how officials in those days would be addressed in cover letters.]

I was excited to read in the Palace Press that you are seeking an **Interpreter of Dreams for Pharaoh.** Let me tell you why I am the person you need:

Dream interpretation: Have been interpreting dreams since I was a youth. Although some are temporarily unfulfilled, my success rate in Egypt has been 100%.

Integrity: Refused improper advances of Potiphar's wife even at my own peril.

Foresight: Realized importance of storing grain during the seven years of plenty to feed people during the seven years of famine.

School of Hard Knocks: I have been cast into a pit by my brothers, sold into slavery, betrayed by my former boss's wife and thrown into prison. Each has been a fruitful, albeit painful, learning experience.

Interpreting dreams for Pharaoh would be very appealing for me. It is a talent I enjoy utilizing and I have enormous respect for a world leader who is like a god to his people. Also, relocating to the palace would pose no logistic problems for me.

It is several millennia too early for resumes, but the Butler knows about my abilities and could render them to you orally. Next week I will contact your office in the palace to see if a meeting can be arranged at your convenience.

Sincerely,
Joseph Jacobson
Joseph Jacobson

The key point to this story is the second paragraph of Joseph's letter. He has addressed each of the criteria noted in the ad explicitly and clearly. For example, the ad cited integrity; Joseph bolds the word "integrity" and then gives an example of it. The third paragraph is also important because it explains why Joseph is interested in the job.

Your well-written cover letter is a partner to your resume that adds value and impact to what you present to an employer. The payoff for the hard work you put into them is being invited to interviews, and preparing for job interviews is the topic of our next chapter.

9

Interview Preparation

MISTAKE #56

Forget what's in your resume and cover letter.

Your resume and cover letter are essential tools for getting you into the interview room. Unfortunately, some people fail to realize that they are also used in the interview room. The interviewer will use the resume and cover letter as a source of questions to ask you. You will not be considered a good candidate if the interviewer knows your resume better than you do. Sometimes, especially at an initial screening, the interviewer will ask you questions simply to gauge the accuracy of your resume and cover letter. If you have forgotten what you wrote, you will lose a great deal of credibility.

Solution

As you prepare for the interview, have a friend ask you "How" and/or "Why" about every line on your resume. When you wrote your resume, you probably thought in terms of what you had done when. Thinking in terms of how and why will give you an additional perspective about your own experiences and accomplishments. What's more, interview questions tend to probe, so you will be preparing for the kinds of questions your interviewer will ask.

MISTAKE #57

Fail to have good examples of your positive characteristics firmly fixed in your mind.

One of the keys to a successful interview is your ability to give specific examples of your positive characteristics (skills, attributes, and behaviors important for doing the job well). Citing illustrative examples is critical whether your interview format is "behavioral," "historical," or something else. Look at the two possible responses Alice might give to the following question:

Interviewer: "Alice, you mentioned that you have good leadership skills. Can you give me an example?"

Alice: (weak response) "Leadership is an important skill. It is the ability to inspire and direct." In this response, Alice has provided a definition but not an example.

Alice: (stronger response) "When I worked at Good Buy Department Store last summer, I was the informal leader of the temporary help. For example, I organized the weekly re-stocking activities so no one individual would be unfairly burdened. Also, I represented the group to our supervisor when we had questions or concerns." Here, she describes her leadership role in a specific situation.

Note that examples don't require having a formal title (e.g., President) or a newsworthy event (e.g., Led the Charge of the Light Brigade).

In another example, Jason might give one of these possible responses to the following question:

Interviewer: "Jason, this position requires a good deal of patience. How would you describe yourself in that regard?"

Jason: (weak) "I take the time to make sure the job is done well and I am patient with others."

Jason: (stronger) "We have seven new members in my neighborhood civic group this year, and I am responsible for getting them involved with supporting our anti-crime effort. Several new people weren't following through on their commitment to attend meetings and participate in a weekly neighborhood walking patrol. It would have been easier to remove them from the membership list, but I prefer to avoid such an extreme step. I have been telling them how important it is to have everyone pitch in to make the safety effort a success. Lately, some of the newer neighbors have gotten involved in a significant way." In this response, Jason has demonstrated patience, using a simple story from his actual civic life. What he related wasn't newsworthy, but it supported his statement that he had patience, and that is the point of the answer.

Solution

Follow these tips for giving good examples:

- **Prepare before the interview:** A list of behaviors that often come up at an interview will be found on pages 38 and 39. In addition, compile a list of skills and characteristics that would be needed to do the job for which you are interviewing. A job description would be a good source for that information. Develop at least two examples demonstrating how you exhibited those behaviors, and be as specific as possible. Providing specific examples enhances your credibility.

- **Clarify:** If you are not sure that your response addressed the question, ask, "Did my example address your question?" or "Would you like another example?"

- **Don't fudge:** Marilyn has never shown leadership skills. To turn this into a positive, she could say, "Actually, I see myself as more of a facilitator and team player. I earn respect and get things accomplished by listening, suggesting, and encouraging."

  Jason doesn't have patience. He could say, "Actually, patience is something I am trying to develop by observing how more patient people deal with situations. For example, I am learning to distinguish between my professional role and my personal feelings when dealing with rude people where I bartend."

- **Consider your sources:** Your examples could come from a job, a volunteer endeavor, or even a class project if you are a student. Examples that took place recently are generally stronger than those from the distant past.

MISTAKE #58

Fail to relate your qualifications to the employer's needs.

The employer will be interested in offering you the job if you are the best available match for the job. Therefore, you want to show that you have the positive characteristics the employer needs.

Solution

Begin your preparation for this question by examining the job description and writing down in a column each skill or characteristic called for. That includes working environment characteristics such as teamwork or travel expectations. To the right of each characteristic, write a brief example indicating where, when, and how you demonstrated that characteristic.

HINT: The inventories of your skills and accomplishments that we discussed in Chapter 6 should give you some good material to help you answer this question.

MISTAKE #59

Forget to inform your references about your job search.

Many employers, former co-workers, and clients will be reluctant to answer any questions about you asked by a potential new employer. There are numerous legal and other professional reasons for this. Yet prospective new employers are edgy about offering employment to someone whose references won't respond. Therefore, if your references are willing to speak about you, that can be a major point in your favor.

Solution

Tell your references that they may be called, what company may be making that call, and that they have your permission to speak freely. Even better, send the reference a letter explicitly giving them permission to talk about you and indicating some of the good things about you that the prospective employer would like to know. This letter will help the reference speak both freely and positively about you. You should include a copy of your resume and cover letter, to help the reference give a knowledgeable assessment of you.

MISTAKE #60

Neglect preparing for a telephone pre-screen.

To control expenses, some companies will conduct at least the initial screening interview over the telephone. The company's minimum goal is to eliminate the obviously inappropriate candidates. Your goal is to avoid being screened out.

Solution

Follow these tips for acing the telephone interview:

If the interview is to be held at a specific time:

- Remember that a telephone interview is a business "meeting" that can have major implications for your career.

- Prepare in advance as you would for any other interview. The fact that the main characters (the interviewer and you) are not able to see each other doesn't change the basic rules.

- Have paper and pencil handy in case you want to take notes.

- Have a list of good questions to ask.

- Get a bit pumped up before the interview begins. Your energy and friendliness in your voice send a message, just as body language would at a face-to-face interview.

- Be prepared for an interview lasting 15 minutes to 30 minutes.

- Have your resume handy so that you can refer to it if necessary.

- Form a mental image of a bright, friendly person on the other end of the telephone.

- Let your voice show enthusiasm.

- Silence is not a bad sign. Don't stumble over yourself trying to end a silence at the other end of the telephone.

If the phone interview is a surprise:

Don't be caught off guard by an unexpected phone interview. Dan sent out ten resumes and followed up with phone calls a week later. So far, he has spoken to ten answering machines. No interview, by telephone or in person, has been arranged. The phone rings one day. It's Denise Johnson from Maybeco calling. She has received Dan's resume and would like to speak with him about it. What should you do if you are in Dan's position?

The surprise telephone interview is a tool that some companies use. There are two reasons. One is expense control, as we noted above. A second is that hiring managers seek to uncover more effectively the real you through an unexpected phone interview. When looking for a new job, you should expect the unexpected. Here's how to ace an unexpected interview:

- Consider the call an unexpected pleasure rather than an intrusion. "It's great to hear from you! I am very interested in your company."

■ Establish a log for each of the companies to which you apply and keep it current. For each company, have some quick notes about their line of business and why you are interested in them. Also jot down the name(s) of contact people. This information may already be available to you if you wrote a good cover letter with each resume you sent. Keep the log by your telephone. If "Denise" calls you, she is probably going to ask you some basic questions about your motivation for that job and what you know about Maybeco. Based on your log, you can answer her questions well enough to avoid being screened out as a candidate not worth pursuing. An alternate approach is to say, "Denise, this is not a good moment for me to speak. Is there a good time for me to get back to you?" The advantage of this approach is that you can buy some time to compose yourself (and prepare yourself) if necessary. The disadvantage is that the delay in conducting the interview will lessen Denise's confidence that she is speaking to the "real" you.

MISTAKE #61

Arrive for a job interview knowing nothing about the employer.

"What do you know about our company?" This is one of the most common questions at an interview. Unfortunately, many people are unprepared to answer it, thus showing a lack of interest and a lack of basic sense.

Solution

You should research the employer before your interview, and become familiar with the following:

■ **The company's line of business.** What does the company produce or what services does it provide?

■ **When the company was established.** How long has it been in business and how has the nature of its business changed over time? It would be very important to know if the present company is the result of a merger or divestiture and/or if the company has changed its name in the last several years.

■ **The company's rank or position in its field or industry,** and its impact/influence on the local economy.

■ **Recent/current events experienced by the company.** You can find this information on the company's website and in the business press.

- **What the company takes particular pride in,** such as its products, services, achievements, and employee relations. This can also be discerned on its website and in the press.

- **Approximate revenue last year** and whether the company was profitable last year and in the recent past. It is more difficult to find out if the company is a partnership or is privately held, because the details may not be found in an easily accessible source such as a web page. However, you may be able to get this information from the office of the attorney general in the state where the company is incorporated or registered. Business magazines have occasional articles on the largest privately held companies in the nation or in a specific geographic area. Because this information is difficult to get, your interviewer is less likely to expect you to have it.

- **Whether the company is regional, national, or international** in nature, as they define themselves.

- **How the company is organized and how many employees it has.** For example, does it have many operating companies under one corporate umbrella?

- **The identity of the company's clients or customers.** If you can't uncover their names, at least try to know what line of business or what business categories are served by the company, or what services it offers.

- **The company's performance as described by the chairman or CEO** in the last annual report or similar public announcement.

- **Challenges the company faces in the near future.** Sometimes information about challenges will be found in the chairman's or CEO's letter to stockholders in the annual report. Both the general press (for stories about legislation, economic conditions, domestic/international political events) and the business press can be good sources.

Since much of the information you need will be found on the company's own website, its website becomes much more of a job-seeking tool for you than a mere resume drop.

MISTAKE #62

Dress inappropriately.

Dressing for an interview is something of a paradox: You won't win the job offer by dressing "correctly," but you can kill your chances by dressing incorrectly. Therefore, your goal with attire is to make it a neutral, non-factor in your interview. The key is to know what kind of attire is appropriate for a job interview.

Solution

Wear standard, sensible business attire, unless you have been told by the company that their interview dress code is business casual. Men should wear a suit, long-sleeved dress shirt, and tie. For women, a suit or skirt (at or below the knee) and blouse would be appropriate. Your shoes should not appear worn, and you should not wear sandals or athletic shoes. Your hair should be arranged in a non-extreme fashion.

If the interview code is business casual, there are a variety of definitions. Generally, a nice pair of slacks, a dress shirt, and a tie would work for men and a simple dress or nice but not fancy blouse and skirt would work for women. If you are uncertain what to wear, ask when you confirm your interview appointment. As a rule of thumb, if you are in doubt, it is safer to dress conservatively.

MISTAKE #63

Arrive late for the interview.

Not being punctual is almost as detrimental as not showing up at all.

Solution

You should plan to arrive about 15 minutes early. That way you can't be late, you won't be unfashionably early, and you will have a chance to take some deep breaths before your interview begins. If you don't know how to reach the interview site, ask for directions when you establish your interview appointment. Assume that traffic will be heavy, there will be construction, and that mass transit will be running late. The worst that can happen if the trip goes smoothly is that you will be very early. In that case, wait until about 15 minutes prior to your interview to enter the office where it will be held.

10

Interview Performance

MISTAKE #64

Fail to be respectful and courteous.

When people are tense as they arrive for an interview, they can inadvertently be rude or disrespectful of company employees in the office—perhaps a receptionist or secretary—while awaiting the interviewer.

Solution

Courtesy doesn't go out of season because of a job interview. Try to treat all those whom you see with the same courtesy and respect you would accord the interviewer. After you leave, the interviewer may ask them what they thought of you.

The same principle applies to other applicants you may meet in the waiting room or at another interview-related function. Think of them as marvelous, talented people with whom you would love to work. From the employer's perspective, how you relate to other applicants may indicate how you would relate to your coworkers. Respect is an obvious winner. In addition, there is nothing that you can do about the other applicants anyway. In America, we don't shoot the competition.

Include the interviewer in your attitude of courtesy and respect. This may seem obvious, but some people go to an interview needlessly combative and overly assertive. While the cause may be sheer anxiety, these are not winning attitudes. Here are some helpful tips:

- **Respect the interviewer's intelligence.** Your interviewer is probably intelligent in general, although understandably ignorant about you in particular. Assuming your interviewer is less intelligent than you will not

71

help you convey a favorable impression, so it is a useless attitude in any event.

Frequently, at least one of your interviewers will be a human resource professional or someone else who is a layman in terms of your field of expertise. In that situation, tailor your remarks as you would when explaining a technical point to anyone you would deal with professionally, such as a customer, a supplier, or a co-worker with another function. Talking over their heads will create a negative impression of you. So will talking down, not to mention declining to discuss a subject because "you wouldn't understand." Remember that your goal is to win the job offer, not to show off how smart you are.

- **Respect the interviewer's age.** Sometimes people are interviewed by a person who is much younger than they are. Statements like "My kids are older than you" or "My, you seem young" give the impression that you don't take the interviewer seriously. Regardless of age, that person will have a voice in determining who gets the job offer. Treat him or her with the respect s/he deserves.

- **Respect the interviewer's prerogatives.** Setting the tone of the interview is the interviewer's prerogative. Perhaps there are policy or practical reasons for being formal or informal. Perhaps it is the interviewer's personal preference. Either way, let it be.

- **Respect the interviewer's space.** In a sense, you are in his/her "territory." Some people will take understandable offense if you put objects on their desk or take other liberties such as moving a chair. Give the interviewer a chance to invite you to sit down. Of course, if you don't get the invitation, sit down anyway.

MISTAKE #65

Fail to communicate a positive attitude.

People who are depressed, downcast, negative, unenthusiastic, or disinterested don't put their best foot forward in the job interview. No one likes "downers," and if you come across this way, you will hurt your chances of a job offer.

Solution

Employers look for candidates who are likable and enthusiastic, with an upbeat, "can-do" attitude. When you are feeling positive about yourself, it is much easier to give positive responses to interview questions, especially those that may hit upon your weaknesses or negatives. Enthusiastic candidates, once on the job, tend to work harder and produce more. In addition, they are more likely to accept the job if offered. This may be a consideration for employers, who would like to close out their vacancy and hire a new employee as soon as possible.

You can communicate your positive attitude in the following ways:

- Research the company thoroughly and communicate some of what you have learned to the interviewer, who will perceive that you are genuinely interested in the company.

- Ask questions that show your interest in the job and the company (see Chapter 12, Questions You Ask the Interviewer).

- Inject energy and vitality into your voice.

- End the interview by asking about the next step or when you might expect to hear from them, thus conveying your sincere interest in the company.

MISTAKE #66

Appear dogmatic and inflexible.

Frequently, an interviewer will ask you about your work style, the type of work environment you prefer, what kind of people you prefer as your colleagues. While you are preparing for the interview, examine your criteria to determine if your attitudes are based on principle or preference. If the subject is a matter of immutable principle, don't be afraid to state it explicitly and stand by it resolutely. On the other had, if it is a matter of personal preference, your response should reveal greater flexibility of mindset.

Solution

The following examples will help you distinguish between principle and preference:

Principles:	Preferences:
Honesty	Bluntness, circumspection
Doing a good job	Workaholic, balanced life
Timeliness	Immediately, before deadline
Courtesy	Formality, informality
Protecting proprietary information	Discussing or avoiding subjects some people find awkward

MISTAKE #67

Overlook the importance of small talk.

Small talk is no small matter. As at most business meetings, your interviewer will probably start with small talk for three reasons. **First,** the interviewer wants to break the ice with you, through chatting about something neither of you finds threatening. **Second,** the interviewer wants to make you less nervous. Meetings are more productive if participants are somewhat relaxed. **Third,** your interviewer may want to see how you present yourself when discussing an apparently mundane topic. S/he is assessing your "people" skills through small talk. If you can't make small talk, you may be less likely to get the job offer.

Solution

The key is to listen to the interviewer's remarks and respond in an upbeat vein. For example, if the interviewer says, "That blizzard is really raising havoc out there," you can follow with a remark like, "It certainly is. I am glad that we were both able to make it in today despite the storm." Avoid a negative or self-centered response like, "It sure is. I got soaked just getting here." Also, avoid a non-communicative response such as a mere "Yes."

    Small talk is not wasted time. It is an opportunity for you to get comfortable in the interview room and to practice listening to what the interviewer says.

    On the downside, small talk has its perils for those who enter the room with a negative outlook or a desire to get cathartic with the interviewer. For example, upon greeting Ralph, the interviewer said, "Ralph, I am glad that you could make it here today despite the blizzard." Ralph responded, "I had a general sense of how to get here, but I got lost. Luckily, your office is closer than I thought or I would have been late." Ralph thus hurt himself in three possible ways: he did not have enough sense to check on directions; his being on time was a matter of luck rather than planning; and he neglected to show interest in the interviewer's commute, perhaps by asking if s/he had also had a hard time driving in the blizzard.

11

Answers to Interview Questions

MISTAKE #68

Fail to respond well to the first substantive question.

After a few minutes of small talk, your interviewer will ask a question that goes to the heart of your interview. Typical opening questions might be:

"Bill, why do you want to leave your current employer?"

"Leslie, please tell me about yourself."

"Alice, tell me about why you chose to become an engineer."

Your response to the opening question is especially important for two reasons. First, the interviewer is likely to ask one or two follow-up questions based on your answer. Second, during the first five minutes, your interviewer will form an impression of you, positive or negative. The rest of the interview serves to confirm or reverse that initial impression. As is human nature, the interviewer will tend to hear what confirms his/her initial impression and to screen out information that conflicts with it. This does not mean that the interview is over in five minutes. It does mean, however, that the early minutes of an interview are especially critical.

Solution

To answer the first question well, include at least one of your positive characteristics that the prospective employer is seeking. That way you are saying something positive about yourself right away and giving the interviewer a good topic for a follow-up question. Let's look at some examples:

Bill (leaving current employer): "I have had a good experience with my current employer and I am proud of my accomplishments. For example, I have developed a loyal staff that is moving ahead in the company. Also, I reduced overhead by 20%, opened up some new markets, and established better ties with existing clients. At this point in my life, I want to take on some fresh challenges. That's what attracted me to your company."

Leslie (describing herself): "People who have seen me work would describe me as a thorough manager who produces an excellent product, on time, even while under pressure. I do this by combining my talents in research and analysis with my interpersonal skills and communication ability. I want to add that I have an excellent staff. Without all of us working together, we couldn't achieve the same results."

Alice (responding to a question about career choice): " I chose to become an engineer for several reasons. One is that I excelled in mathematics and the natural sciences. In addition, I enjoyed reading engineering magazines before I even started college. Once I entered the engineering program, the group projects we worked on in class were exciting. In my favorite project, we made some interesting observations about the impact of gravity on small bridges. That is one of the reasons I am excited to be interviewing with Build-A-Bridge Associates."

MISTAKE #69

Be unprepared for behavioral questions.

When a position needs to be filled, many interviewers like to ask questions directly addressed to the types of behaviors that are important in doing that job well. The theory is that your past behaviors are a good predictor of your future behaviors. For example, if the position requires teamwork skills, you will be asked a question about teamwork, perhaps as straightforward as, "Shelley, tell me about how you have worked on a team during the last twelve months." The question could become even more specific. The interviewer might continue, "Specifically, tell me what the objective of the team was, how you organized yourselves, and what your particular role was."

Behavioral questions are very specific as to their topic, so they do not provide much latitude for introducing your own agenda or side-stepping the intent of the interviewer. Also, your response to a behavioral question is especially important since the topic goes directly to your ability to do the job.

Solution

The behavioral mode of questions brings some advantages to you. **First**, although you cannot predict the wording of the questions, you can prepare beforehand for the subject matter. Look at the job description carefully. If it contains words like analytical, communication, deadline, etc, you should definitely prepare responses indicating that you have demonstrated those very behaviors in your current job or in some fairly recent experience. **Second**, prepare responses about common characteristics and behaviors that are generic to many jobs using the table on pages 38 and 39.

Here are some examples of behavioral questions:

"Describe a time when you were faced with problems of stress at work that tested your coping skills. What did you do?"

"Can you tell me about a specific occasion when you conformed to a policy even though you did not agree with it?"

"Give me an example of a time when you were able to communicate successfully with another person, even when that individual may not have liked you personally."

"Describe a situation in which others within your organization depended upon you. What did you do in your last summer in order to be effective with your organization and planning? Be specific."

"Tell me about a situation in the past year when you had to deal with a very upset customer or co-worker (or fellow student). How did you handle that situation?"

"Give me an example of a time when you had to be relatively quick in coming to a decision."

"Give me an example of an important goal you set and your process in reaching it."

"Think about a time when you exercised a leadership role. How did you become the leader? What challenges did you face? What did you achieve?"

"Describe a problem you solved on your own and a problem you solved working with others."

"How do you go about managing your time to accomplish your goals? How do you set priorities?"

MISTAKE #70

Prepare poorly for reflective questions.

Reflective questions are also intended to probe whether you are a good fit for the job, but they tend to be more open-ended.

Solution

Here are some reflective questions you should think about before your interview:

- **Why do you think that this company should hire you?**

   This is really a great question from your perspective because it gives you a chance to talk about some of the skills and characteristics that would make you a good match for the job.

- **"Why did you apply for this position?"**

   This is a good chance to give reasons why you are interested in doing the job and in working for that company specifically. If a friend of yours in the company told you about the job opening, you could mention that. If you have been looking for an opportunity like this one, you could say that.

- **"How would a co-worker describe you in three words?"**

   Think professionally. Choose three characteristics that would make you a good employee. As always, have examples ready to support what you say. Words like honest, reliable, fun to be with may be appropriate to this answer even though they generally don't appear in a job description.

- **"What was the most difficult decision you ever had to make? How did you make that decision?"**

   Answer in terms of a difficult decision, not necessarily the *most* difficult. Superlative terms like most and least need not be taken literally. Also, remember that the question refers to professional decisions. It is generally best to keep very personal decisions, such whether to get married, out of the interview. Note that sometimes a reflective question is really similar to a behavioral one.

- **"Looking back over the last few years, is there anything you wish that you had done differently?"**

   Usually there is something we would have done differently. That is one value of experience.

- "Is there anything about this job that you might find unattractive?"

Usually there is something you might find unattractive and you should be aware of that if you have thought seriously about the job. However, it is still a good idea to accentuate the positive. Start by saying what you would like about the job. Then mention some factor that you might find unappealing. Indicate that you want the job, that every job has aspects that may be unappealing, and that you understand the need to do every aspect of the job well, not just those parts that you enjoy.

MISTAKE #71

Be uncertain how to answer a hypothetical question.

You may be asked a situational question framed in a "what-if" format. For example, "What would you do if an employee whom you are managing is performing up to standard, but not up to his/her abilities?" or "What would you do if a proposal you worked on for over three months was severely criticized by your manager?" Some line managers still ask this type of question, although fewer human resources professionals utilize it.

Solution

Here is what you can do:

- **Actualize the hypothetical.** You can discuss an actual situation. For example, "I was in a situation like that once. Let me tell you how I handled it...." This approach has two advantages. First, it may be easier to handle because it is less abstract. Second, a real situation may be more useful for the questioner to evaluate.

- **Consider what you would need to know.** Another approach is to think in terms of the process that you would follow to solve the problem: What would you need to know? What would be your priorities? What external interests would you have to consider? Let's see how Bill answered a hypothetical question about conflicting demands on his time:

  "There are several things that I would need to know, to resolve this conflict. First, can I get either client to change appointment times without the loss of their business? If not, my own priority would be to satisfy the existing larger client because it is important to be pragmatic. I assume that I am being evaluated on total business, not new customers. However, I need to take the company's interest into account. Is there any reason why the potential client is more important than I think? Perhaps we need to gain exposure with clients in their field of business."

■   **It won't happen because...** It is possible that you will be asked about a hypothetical situation that you would work hard to prevent. For example, "Tell me what you would do if you had two deadlines to meet simultaneously and had time to complete only one." If neither of the two types of response noted above works for you, it is possible to respond like this: "That situation has never happened to me because I always plan ahead and put my ducks in a row long before a deadline looms. Let me give you an example...."

MISTAKE #72

Talk about your weaknesses.

At some point in the interview you may be asked to identify some of your weaknesses. Since we are all human, we all have them. However, there is no way you can win points in your favor by reciting a long list of shortcomings. On the other hand, denying that you have weaknesses would destroy your credibility, and citing your Fifth Amendment protection against self-incrimination would lead people to think that you have something to hide. Therefore, the best you can do is to neutralize the issue.

Solution

There are three possible approaches you can take.

1.   **The classic:** Refer to a "weakness" that is really a strength. An example would be your determination to complete all your assignments by or before the deadline. Sometimes the interviewer will follow up and ask for another weakness. Then you could use the minimizer or the open counter.

2.   **The minimizer:** Pick an attribute that is not essential to the job being discussed. For example, you might say "Although I have facility in using computers, I would not do well as a programmer."

3.   **The open counter:** Remember that you want to address the question and should always try to avoid an argument. You can express your openness to addressing any weaknesses of concern to the interviewer, but ask if he or she could specify what potential weakness they would like you to discuss. For example, "Everybody has their weaknesses, but I would like to address those skills or characteristics that are of interest to you. Is there anything about me that you would like me to address?"

MISTAKE #73

Engage in puffery and lying.

Stick with the facts and let them speak for you. "Last year, out of a district with 23 managers, I was the number one sales manager in terms of generating profit" is an impressive statement. "I am the best manager in the entire district" is not. The difference is that the first statement is factual while the second is an opinion.

Solution

Don't exaggerate, let alone lie. If you were the number three sales manager, don't claim to have been number one or two. Nobody expects a candidate who can walk on water, but everybody insists upon a candidate who is honest.

MISTAKE #74

Praise yourself instead of stating your accomplishments.

Beth was asked why she should be hired. "I am the best candidate you could possibly hire," she responded. There are several problems with this response. **First,** Beth was in no position to evaluate any of the other applicants. **Second,** bragging about herself did not reflect positively on her. **Third,** Beth could have given a compelling answer, but didn't. In the solution below we will focus on this third point—giving a compelling answer.

Solution

If true, Beth could have said something like the following:

> "My current manager, Doris Greene, has called me the best employee she has ever had in the position I currently hold." Stated this way, Beth would be utilizing a kind of third-party testimonial that tends to be both impressive and credible. She should then proceed to indicate why Ms. Greene spoke so highly of her, quantifying her achievements if possible. "You need a person who can sell to large, institutional clients. Last year, I was ranked number one in that category by my present company."

In this response, Beth allowed her recent success do the talking.

MISTAKE #75

Criticize other applicants.

Aaron was asked at his interview, "Why should we hire you instead of the 16 other candidates who are going through this process?" His response was quite inappropriate: "Unlike your other applicants, I am not one of these people who..."

Never badmouth anybody! That includes trying to make yourself look good by casting others in a negative light.

Solution

The question should be seen simply as an opportunity for Aaron to present some of his own selling points. He should have responded something like this: "I am sure that you are interviewing a number of very talented people. Many people in my field would want to work for a great company like Thisco. The reason you should hire me is..." Stated this way, Aaron would have praised the company (a moderate amount of flattery doesn't hurt) and would have said some positive, job-related things about himself. His very approach to the question would show that he had tact and was likely to be a team player.

Never think of other applicants as competitors, let alone enemies. Instead, view them as very talented people whom you would be proud to call colleagues.

MISTAKE #76

Give rambling answers.

You may have heard the story about the fellow who was asked, "What time is it?" and responded with a long discourse on the history of time keeping and its significance for Western civilization. That type of rambling answer may be fatal to your job chances because it tests the listener's patience and doesn't actually answer the question s/he asked.

Solution

Here are strategies to avoid rambling:

- **Pause.** No one expects you to respond to a question in real time as though you were a computer. Part of your value to the employer is your ability to think before, rather than after, speaking. So, take a moment to collect your thoughts before responding to a question. If you need more than a few seconds, you could say, "That is an interesting question. Let me think about that for a moment." The very act of pausing may help you convey the impression of being a thoughtful person, and that can't hurt. There are some additional advantages. First, your pause is helpful to the interviewer because it gives him/her a chance to switch from speaking mode to listening mode. Second, your pause will stop you from annoying the interviewer by interrupting her/him. Third, you are more likely to convey sincerity and less likely to appear pre-programmed.

- **Plan.** Use the time of your pause to summarize the essence of the question for yourself and to outline in your head a few points you want to bring out. That rudimentary road map helps you stay focused and on topic.

- **Ask if in doubt.** One reason people ramble is that they try to force too much content into a single answer. Think in terms of an answer that consists of a few sentences, not a paragraph or two. If you are not sure that you have answered the question completely, you can always ask the interviewer, "Would you like me to tell you more about that?"

MISTAKE #77

Fail to answer the question.

Some people say a lot when measured by word count, but convey little that is relevant. This is because they haven't answered the question that was asked.

Solution

Two pointers will help you avoid that mistake: **First, know how to listen.** Only by listening carefully to the question is it possible to give a responsive answer. In particular, listen to the intent of the question. What is it that the interviewer really wants to know? Here is a short parable that may be helpful:

The Creation Epic: An Interviewing Perspective

In the Beginning, the Creator considered how best to fashion humans. There were many things to take into account—muscles, circulation, growth potential and spiritual development. The Creator also determined that humans' very structure would be a lesson in how to do things right. Therefore, the Creator determined that humans should have:

Two ears: to emphasize the importance of listening.

A brain: placed deliberately between the ears to help humans think about what they heard others saying.

A mouth: for speaking, but only after hearing and thinking first.

The Creator looked upon humans and saw that they were good, especially for interviewing. And thus it is that "Listen, Think, Respond" became an interviewing creed for all time.

Let's look at the question Leslie was asked in MISTAKE #57. When the interviewer asked, "Tell me about yourself," Leslie realized that the interviewer was referring to job-related aspects of her life, especially those that might be reasons to offer her a job. A discussion of her family, hobbies, or golf handicap would address the literal sense of the question but not its intent. Leslie's answer thus focused on her job.

Second, if you are not sure about the intent of the question, ask. You could say, "I want to make sure that I understand your question properly. Are you interested in knowing more about my writing skills?" Remember that an interview is a business meeting between equals. At a business meeting, you would clarify a question if necessary before giving your response.

Don't be afraid to give an honest answer. Sometimes people talk around a question hoping that the interviewer won't notice. This is a mistake. The interviewer probably will notice. The sense that you have something to hide will only prompt more probing questions. What's worse, if the interviewer thinks that you are lying, that is more likely to end your prospects of a job offer than the underlying problem. Since whatever is troublesome about the question will not simply go away, address it. However, you can add a possible resolution. For example, "No, I haven't had any substantive experience with supervising others. I do think I would be good at it, however, because I am a good listener, a patient person, and one who can see the bigger picture."

MISTAKE #78

Discuss money before being offered the job.

In most cases, answering the interviewer's questions about compensation before you have the job offer is not to your advantage. For example, if s/he asks, "How much do you expect to get paid?," any specific number you give works against you. If your salary expectation exceeds the figure the company is planning to pay, you may be ruled out of the running. On the other hand, if the figure you mention is too low, you may be considered lacking in self-confidence or your statement may be used against your interests if you are offered the job and want to negotiate the salary. So what should you do?

Solution

There are several possibilities.

1. **Not an issue (at least yet).** You could respond something like this: "What I am most interested in is taking the right job with the right company. I am sure that your compensation package is competitive with the market. If you decide to offer me this position, and I hope that you do, I am sure that we can reach an agreement on compensation that makes everybody happy."

2. **Give a range.** Try not to give a specific number, but answering with a salary range that you know is reasonable makes sense: "I haven't thought about this in detail yet, but a salary between the middle $50's and middle $60's seems to be about right." If you have done your pre-interview "homework," you will have researched salaries for that position and thus will be able to give a range that you know is reasonable.

3. **If the interviewer is persistent.** Sometimes an interviewer will come at you again after you have given one of the answers above. In that case you could respond," I am sure that your compensation package is a good one. What are you planning to offer your best candidate?"

12

Questions You Ask the Interviewer

MISTAKE #79

Ask poor or inappropriate questions.

When employers evaluate you as a job candidate, your questions to the interviewer are a major consideration. Unfortunately, many people do not realize this and thus ask poorly conceived questions, or even none at all.

> Just how important are your questions in the employer's evaluation of you as a job candidate? A few years ago, I surveyed employers across the United States. Over half of the responding employers said that your questions are as important as your answers to their questions. Most of the remaining employers said that your answers are less important, but still significant. A few said your answers are actually more important.

Typically, five or ten minutes prior to the end of the interview, the interviewer will ask you if you have any questions. Your questions reveal a lot about you. For example:

- How seriously you are thinking about the pragmatics of the job, and how well you understand what the job is about.

- What is important to you, and what your expectations are.

- Your ability to connect general situations to that company's specific reality.

- How much research you did on the company.

- Your degree of common sense and intellectual curiosity.

- Your energy level and communication skills.

- How well prepared you are (or would be in the future) for a business meeting.

- Your level of maturity (especially if you are a recent college graduate).

Thus, your questions need to present you in the most favorable light.

Solution

There are two steps to asking good questions. First, become fully familiar with the "Five Rules for Asking a Question." By following these five rules, you will come across as a person who is sincere, prepared, and thorough. You will also get more useful answers.

Rule #1: You care about the topic.

If you are not interested in the topic, don't ask about it. An insincere question undermines one of the most important bases for your success, namely the interviewer's trust in your integrity as a person. However, if you do care about the subject, move on to the next rule.

Rule #2: Read about, thought about.

Make sure that you have researched the topic before you ask about it. Preparation for your interview, like preparation for any business meeting, reflects strongly on your professional competence. It also reflects on the seriousness of your interest. It is a good idea to refer to your research when presenting your question. For example, you could start your question by saying, *"I read on your website that..."*

Rule #3: The answer is not found in some obvious place.

You would probably feel embarrassed if you asked for information about the company's history and it is given on the homepage of the company's website. Double-check the obvious sources (website, recruiting literature, job description, or recent issues of business publications to make sure that your question isn't already answered.

Rule #4: Don't let your questions throw up barriers to your candidacy.

Make sure that the question you are considering doesn't raise barriers to getting the job offer. For example, let's say that you ask "Is relocation a necessary part of the job?" The very question may raise doubts about your ability to relocate. If you need to ask about this topic, preface your question with, *"I know that relocation is often part of a good career and I am prepared to relocate as necessary. Could you tell me how often I might be asked to relocate in a five- or ten-year period? When might the first relocation occur?"*

Rule #5: Ask questions that are appropriate for your interviewer.

Consider your question in light of the other person's role in the company. It makes sense to ask about strategy if you are speaking with a middle- or senior-level employee. Asking an entry-level employee why s/he chose to join this company after college is also reasonable. But reversing the questions would make little sense and might embarrass both you and the interviewer.

The second step to asking good questions is to know what topics your questions should be focused on:

1. **The job itself:** Ask at least two questions about the nature of the work you would be doing.

    "When you think about people who tend to do well in this job, what kind of qualities do they typically have?"

    "I read on your website that new employees spend five weeks in training before starting hands-on in their new job. Could you tell me more about that? I am especially interested in knowing if the training is given by outside consultants or in-house managers. Also, do people in any given training class tend to be identified as members of that class afterwards?"

    "I certainly intend to work hard and to prove my value to this company. If there is a formal evaluation system, are evaluations given at specific intervals and would my immediate manager conduct the evaluation?"

    "I am a good Web designer and love what I do. At the same time, I realize that the company won't succeed if the website doesn't work in tandem with the marketing plan or if the website absorbs too much capital. Can you tell me how the different departments at Gadgetco work together?"

    "Could you tell me if senior managers invite ideas and feedback from middle managers or even entry level employees?"

2. **The company:** At least one good question about the nature of the company, its products and/or services, its future challenges.

"A recent article in the Wall Street Journal suggested that it is time for companies like Yourco to be more concerned with profit margins than with market share. Can you tell me if Yourco has any plans to shift its priorities in that direction?"

"There are number of players in Yourco's market. Yet you have been successful in maintaining and even expanding your client base. What is it about Yourco that makes customers choose you?"

"The Robert Wrench Kit seems to have struck a responsive chord with the workshop market. How did the idea develop to package the wrenches in their own toolbox?"

"Yourco's chairman, Mr. Young, indicated that for the next three years cost cutting would be a major priority. Do you feel that the department will be budgeted enough resources to meet its performance goals?"

3. **The industry or profession:** You may want to ask about events in the industry (e.g., consumer products) or profession (e.g., public accounting) of which the prospective employer is a part.

    "Standard & Poors Industry Surveys reported that the industry as a whole is becoming more export oriented. Do you think that trend can be sustained in light of competition from low-wage but technologically competent countries?"

    "Industry Monthly predicted that there would be a consolidation of companies within this industry, resulting in fewer but larger companies. Do you think that consolidation would put new product development on hold, or would it lead to increased availability of resources for that purpose?"

    "In what way, if any, has the recently enacted Sarbanes-Oxley legislation changed the way that the public accounting profession relates to its clients?"

4. **External influences:** Consider asking how events such as pending legislation, development of new technologies, or international situations are affecting the industry, company, or the specific job for which you are being interviewed.

    "There is some talk in Congress about loosening consumer product safety regulation. While complying with regulations can be a burden to companies in terms of cost, it can also increase consumer confidence in products. On balance, how has consumer product safety legislation impacted on Yourco?"

    "Russia has been increasing its oil exports and some of the Islamic republics in the Caucasus region may do so soon as well. If the result is a lower price for a barrel of crude, do you think that there will still be a strong market for Yourco's expensive but highly-fuel efficient car?"

Sometimes an interviewer may not ask you if you have any questions. You can initiate a question without being invited, but three caveats are in order.

First, be careful about *starting* the interview with your own question. Some interviewers prefer to ask the initial questions in order to feel in control. Therefore, prudence suggests not asking questions until you have answered a few.

Second, use your common sense. If your interviewer seems less than pleased with questions you ask without an invitation, hold further questions until they are solicited.

Third, it is a good idea to explicitly link your questions with the ongoing discussion. Use an introductory phrase like, "We've been discussing widgets. I would like to clarify something you mentioned about widgets at Yourco."

MISTAKE #80

Fail to articulate your thoughts well.

A job interview can be a very stressful situation. When you are in an interview, you will naturally feel very nervous and may have trouble articulating your thoughts to the interviewer when s/he asks you if you have any questions.

Solution

- Write out your questions and bring them to the interview, preferably in a handy binder or on index cards.

- If you feel you need to refer to your notes, say, "I have written down a number of questions. Would you mind if I refer to my notes?" Politeness doesn't go out of season.

- However, don't *read* your questions. Just look at your notes to jog your memory, then face the interviewer and ask the question. Reading your questions reduces their effectiveness.

MISTAKE #81

Pose your questions badly.

Some people seriously hurt their candidacy by asking questions that inadvertently convey their shortcomings to the interviewer.

Solution

Here are five poison pills to avoid:

1. **Me first:** Some questions make you seem self-centered. The worst offenders are those who ask about salary or fringe benefits, especially at a first interview. Hold those questions until *after* the job offer has been extended.

2. **Insecurities:** Most people feel insecure about something, but exposing a job-related insecurity could really get in your way. Worst offenders in this group are questions such as "How secure is this job?" and "May I take time off at Thanksgiving and the holidays?

3. **Weaknesses:** Most interview books tell you how to finesse the dreaded *"Tell me about your weaknesses"* question. Unfortunately, many job candidates *reveal* their weaknesses through their questions. For example, *"Would I have to meet a lot of deadlines?"* gives the impression that you have trouble with deadlines. If so, this is not a topic you wish to initiate.

4. **Tone of communication:** Sometimes it is the tone you take, instead of the topic under discussion, that can hurt your candidacy. Your tone can be a matter of your voice or of the words you choose, so you need to be careful of both. *"Why don't you guys get with it and use the Internet more?"* would be a good example of a question striking the wrong tone.

5. **Subject already discussed:** A good way to expose yourself as a poor listener is to ask a question as if the topic is new, when in fact it has already been thoroughly discussed. The right thing to do is this: Summarize briefly what has already been discussed on a subject, then ask a question to clarify what you heard or to pursue another aspect of that topic.

HINT: "No questions" is not an option. Asking good questions does require work. Can you politely turn down the opportunity to ask questions? Only at the peril of losing a job opportunity! Employers are nearly unanimous in saying that not asking questions will hurt your chances of getting a job offer.

MISTAKE #82

Ask questions at the wrong stage of the interview process.

There are a few questions that I encourage you *not* to initiate until you have the offer in hand. These are questions that will never help you get the job, but could cost you the job offer instead, if you ask them at the wrong time.

Solution

Know what questions not to ask until you have the job offer in hand.

1.   **Compensation, including your salary, vacation, benefits etc**. A compensation-based question doesn't indicate anything positive about you and is in any event, premature. No one has offered you the job yet, so what point does the question serve? It is not information you really need to know yet. Further, many interviewers regard asking this question at an interview as a tasteless example of a self-centered attitude.

On the other hand, be prepared to respond if the *interviewer* initiates the question of compensation with you. The following examples between John and an interviewer should be helpful.

Interviewer: "John, can you tell me what your salary expectations are?"

John: "I am sure that your company is at least competitive in terms of salary, and my expectations are in line with that."

or

"I am expecting something between the high $50's and the low $60's."

or

"That's a good question. What are you planning to pay your best candidates?"

You can't advance your candidacy with your answer to a compensation question, so just try to neutralize it by giving an appropriately unspecific response. Once the job is offered, you can negotiate compensation from a position of strength, so try to defer any detailed discussions until then.

A partial exception is in the case of a commissioned rather than salaried position. Sales jobs are a typical example. In a sales situation, the desire to earn a high income is an unambiguous virtue. After all, the more money you make, the more money your manager makes. Therefore, at an interview for a sales job you could respond, *"It's hard to say how much money I would make in the first year, but by my third year I expect to be making at least $60,000."*

2. **Conditions of employment, such as starting date, flex time, travel, and relocation.** Let's say you ask, *"Is flextime a possibility?"* The question says nothing positive about you, so it doesn't help you get the offer. On the other hand, your question may raise doubts about your willingness to work the typical schedule. For many jobs, that could eliminate you from consideration for the position.

Once an employer has decided that you are the right person for the job, s/he is more likely to accommodate your preferences about starting dates, work hours, and perhaps even travel and relocation. You may raise these questions *after* you have the offer in hand. Of course, if you are asked about these subjects at an interview, give an honest, thoughtful response, but try to avoid coming across as self-centered.

13

Interview Follow Through

MISTAKE #83

Forget the important follow-through steps.

Michael just had an interview with Wonderfulco, the company of his dreams. "It went well," he thought, "Now I can relax and see what happens." Michael was about to make a big mistake. Failing to follow through after a job interview conveys a lack of seriousness about the job and suggests that the candidate might not follow through on responsibilities if he did get the job. Further, the job seeker who doesn't follow through overlooks an opportunity to make himself a more attractive candidate to a prospective employer.

Solution

These are the follow-though steps you should take:

- **After the interview, take notes.** As soon as you have left the office where you had the interview and have privacy, take notes on what transpired at the interview. What was the first question, how did you answer? What was of most interest to the interviewer in terms of following up on your answers or in term of repeating questions in different ways. What were the interviewer's answers to your questions? Was any next step indicated at the end of the interview? What made you feel comfortable or uncomfortable about the interview? What were the names and positions of those whom you met at the prospective place of employment? These notes will help you do well if you are invited to a follow-up interview, and/or to prepare for interviews with other companies.

- **Send a thank you to each interviewer.** You should send an email thank-you note later that same day and a hardcopy thank you through the regular U.S. mail as soon as possible.

- **Update those who have helped you.** Let those who have been helping you in your job search, especially those who helped you obtain that particular interview, know how the interview went.

HINT: Keep up your job search. Sometimes after a good interview people relax so much that they forget to continue full steam with their job search. An interview, even a good one, shouldn't cause you to pause in your search. Remember that an interview is not a job offer.

MISTAKE #84

Treat a follow-up interview the same as the previous interview.

For most positions, the first interview serves as a screening. If the employer thinks that there is a good possibility of a match, you will probably be invited to a follow-up interview. This is generally the interview when the employer will make a definitive decision on whether or not to offer you the job

The follow-up interview is even more serious for the company because it is more expensive to conduct and because the goal is to identify the candidate to whom the job will be offered. In fact, some companies call this stage the <u>hiring</u> interview. If you think that the follow-up interview will just be more of the same, you won't be properly prepared.

Solution

Therefore, you should be familiar with the different ways in which a follow-up interview is conducted.

- **The structure of the interview process.** Typically, you will be interviewed by a number of people and the process frequently takes the better part of a workday. Each interview may now last for an hour, and you are likely to be interviewed by people at different levels of authority within the company. Your prospective manager (the boss) will probably be one of them. At some companies, you may be in an interview room with a panel of several interviewers. We discuss panel interviews in MISTAKE #85.

■ **Questions you will be asked.** Some of the questions you will be asked may be new. For example, "How will you evaluate your job offers to determine which one to accept?" The point of this question is to flatter you a bit but, more importantly, to probe your values. Since some time has passed since your initial interview, you may be asked if you have done additional preparation for the next stage of interviews: "What have you learned about our company since your initial interview?

Other questions will reflect notes taken by the interviewer during your screening interview, indicating topics that require validation or more intensive probing. Still others may reveal the specific interests of the various interviewers.

HINT: That's one reason the notes you took after the initial interview are so important.

■ **Questions you will ask your interviewers.** The questions you ask will now need to be fine-tuned and must address the professional interests and level of authority of the interviewers. Let's look at some examples:

For an interviewer who has just recently joined the company:

"Why did you choose X Corp.? Do you feel comfortable telling me why you preferred X Corp to other companies?"

"How would you describe the working atmosphere at X Corp?" (Hint: It is best to ask an open-ended question because you will learn more from the response. If you are asked to clarify your question, you could be more specific, "Do you find the atmosphere to be formal or informal?")

For someone who holds a position similar to the one you are interviewing for:

"What are the most satisfying or least satisfying parts of your job?"

"How does your position relate to other functions at X Corp?"

"Where do you see yourself in X Corp in three to five years?"

For a person with senior management responsibility:

"How is X Corp positioning itself to deal with the current economic slowdown (or expansion)?"

"What does it takes in terms of outlook, skill, and determination to be a manager with this company?"

"If you were to make a sound decision that results in a worse-than-antici-pated outcome, will you be evaluated more on the soundness of the deci-sion or on the disappointment of the outcome?"

For a person who works in an area (e.g., engineering, marketing, store, head-quarters) not directly part of the area for which you are interviewing:

"What are some of the challenges you face in your (division or functional area)?"

"In what ways does (your function) work along with (my function)? Are there any aspects of the relationship that you would like to see improved?"

"How has your function changed over the past four years or so?"

MISTAKE #85

Be unprepared for a panel interview.

Sometimes an interview involves more than one person in the room in addition to you. Marilyn entered the interview room and was a bit startled. Nervous to begin with, she nearly panicked when she saw a panel of five interviewers. From the company's per-spective, the panel brings together people from different functions within the company and/or different levels of authority. This can be a good way to have different ears hear and evaluate the same answers. Also, there is less pressure on any individual inter-viewer to maintain the flow of questions and make notes of the responses.

Solution

These are strategies you should adopt:

- **When responding to a question, look first at the questioner.** After a moment or two, you should bring the other members of the panel into your response by looking at them also.

- **Direct your questions to more than just one panel member.** If you pre-pared your questions well (See MISTAKE #79), this shouldn't be a prob-lem.

- **It is likely that one member of the panel has been designated as the "bad guy"** and will ask especially difficult or even harsh questions. You should not take this personally or act defensively. In fact you could even begin your response by saying, "That is a very good question…"

- **You should not yield to the temptation to focus on the friendliest looking face** on the panel. This is especially true if that friendly face happens to be of the same race, ethnic group, age, or gender as you are. The other panel members are liable to take offense and wonder if you are capable of relating well to all your potential co-workers and managers.

MISTAKE #86

Terminate an interview process too soon.

Some people, perhaps subconsciously, leave an interview not feeling great about the job. Since interviews under most circumstances are stressful, this ill feeling may be related to the stress rather than to the job. Unfortunately, Janice had this experience. "I will never work in that place," she said to herself. In that frame of mind, she didn't follow up with an enthusiastic thank-you letter or respond favorably when invited to a follow-up interview. Subsequently, a friend took that job and loved it. By rejecting a prospective job based solely on the interview experience, Janice needlessly lost an opportunity that might have worked well for her.

Solution

Here are some guidelines to follow, especially regarding follow-up visits:

- **No way! Really?** If you are 100 percent sure, positively, absolutely, that there is no way that you would accept a job offer from that company then don't go to the interview. On the other hand, if there is any chance that you might want the job, definitely go. Remember that the interviewer is not the company. Perhaps you didn't like your first stage interviewer. Don't let a half-hour experience with one individual close out further consideration of a potential career opportunity.

  On a personal note, after my screening interview, I told my wife that I would definitely never work for that employer. Somehow, I accepted the invitation to a follow-up visit, even though it involved a significant trip. I am now employed at precisely the place I had dismissed out of hand initially. A second look can dramatically change your perspective.

- **Don't count birds in the bushes.** Don't turn down a follow-up interview on the assumption that another company with which you have interviewed is going to offer you a job. There is no job offer until the company has explicitly made it, in writing. Praise for your capabilities and the potential with the company are not the equivalent of a job offer.

  Unless there is a risk to your current job or an inordinate investment of time, don't bail out of an interviewing process until it ends in a rejection or a job offer. The exception would be if pursuing the process with a specific company would be unethical.

- **Ethical considerations.** Rick was thinking about going to the follow-up interview because he looked forward to the trip and to staying in a nice hotel. If that was the only reason in Rick's mind, he shouldn't go. It would be unethical to waste the company's time and money. Also, remember that only a limited number of people can be invited to a follow-up interview. If this job opportunity is an absolute non-starter for Rick, he should realize that another candidate could really benefit from the chance at this position.

A change in your level of interest can occur in the other direction as well. At his initial interview, David had sincerely told the interviewer that he wanted the job. In the context of the interview, he was telling the truth. Several weeks later, he had a different perspective on the situation and preferred to end his relationship with that company. At that stage of the process, it was not unethical for David to change his mind, thank the company, and withdraw from consideration for the position. Further, no one should think that he was lying at the interview.

14

The Job Offer

MISTAKE #87

Fail to stall for more time.

Larry just received a job offer from Secondchoice, Inc., a nice company to be sure, but not his first choice. Secondchoice asked him to respond to their offer within two weeks. Primo Company won't let him know about a job offer for at least a month. Larry would like to be ethical in his dealings with Secondchoice while still hoping for an offer from Primo.

This is what Larry should definitely NOT do:

- **Accept the bird in the hand.** He should not despair about the timing issue and accept Secondchoice on the theory that a bird in the hand is worth two in the bush. He may regret that later.

- **Accept in bad faith.** Larry should not accept the Secondchoice offer on the theory that he can always change his mind (and his answer) later. That would be completely unethical, analogous to accepting an offer of marriage while still be open to marriage proposals from other suitors. Secondchoice would consider the position filled, notify other candidates with their regrets and plan on Larry's arrival. That would be a very expensive proposition for Secondchoice if Larry subsequently retracted his acceptance. Further, people talk and what goes around comes around. Larry might find that he had poisoned his future opportunities in that profession or industry.

Solution

Stalling can be done in a professional and ethical way. Larry should call Myrna, the person at Soundchoice who signed his offer letter, and say, "I am excited about your job offer. However, this is a very serious decision for me to make. You asked for a decision by May 30. Can we move the decision date back to June 15? That extra time would be very important to me." If Myrna says, "Larry, we really hope that you will accept the offer, but if you need extra time take it," Larry's timing conflict is resolved. Of course, he should send her an e-mail thanking her for extending the decision date until June 15. If, on the other hand, she says, "Larry, we really want you, but we can't move that decision date. We need to hear from you by May 30," Larry moves to the next step.

He calls Sheila, his contact person at Primo. "Sheila, I have enjoyed meeting with you and all the other people at Primo. I am excited about the possibility of working for you. However, I have a timing problem. Another company has made me a nice offer but their outside deadline for a decision is May 30. If Primo is going to offer me the position we discussed, is there any way that you can let me know by May 29? Primo is my first choice, but I can't let the other opportunity pass me by because of timing."

If she tells him Primo will get back to him by May 29, his timing problem is solved. If she says that no decision will be made before June 15, he still has a timing problem. However, he now knows that he is not so important to either company that they will be flexible about dates. Especially in regard to Primo, Larry may want to reconsider how attractive that company is to him.

MISTAKE #88

Compare job offers to each other rather than to your requirements.

Hopefully, your job search will result in more than one job offer. (Even if it doesn't, there is an implicit choice between a new offer and your current job or a job offer and having no job.) Some people drive themselves crazy comparing one offer to another. Even worse, the conclusions the job seeker draws may not necessarily reflect his/her own best interests.

Solution

The productive thing is to compare each job offer to what you want. The following exercise will help you evaluate a job offer.

- Identify your priorities—what you want most in a job.

- Rank your priorities.

■   Assess the degree to which a particular job satisfies your priorities.

Step 1:   List the priorities that are important to you in a job. Your list can be as long as you wish. A table of common priorities will be found on page 103.

Step 2:   Allocate 100 points among the priorities on your list. The more important the priority, the more points you should assign to it.

Step 3:   Evaluate the degree to which the job offer you are considering meets your priorities. Assign a value from .00 (doesn't meet your priorities at all) to 1.00 (meets your priorities completely).

Step 4:   Multiply the number from Step 2 ("100 points") by the number in Step 3. Add the products of your multiplication to determine your evaluation of the job offer against the priorities that are important to you.

EXAMPLE:

Step 1:

Larry's Priorities

1 Compensation
2 Location
3 Starting date
4 Mobility
5 Comfort with co-workers

Step 2:

Take 100 points and allocate them among the priorities

Compensation	25
Location	30
Starting date	10
Mobility	20
Comfort with co-workers	15

Steps 3 & 4:

To what degree does a particular job fulfill Larry's priorities?

.95	Compensation	25 =	23.75
.50	Location	30 =	15.
1.00	Starting date	10 =	10.
.70	Mobility	20 =	14.
.20	Comfort with co-workers	15 =	3.
		TOTAL:	65.75

If the answer seems uncomfortable to you, re-examine the first three steps:

- Is your list of important criteria *accurate* and *complete?*

- When you allocated the 100 points, did you *accurately* rank your criteria and give each criterion an appropriate weight?

- When you assessed the *degree* to which a specific job offer meets your criteria, did you assign appropriate weights?

Make any changes necessary and re-calculate the result.

Common Job Priorities
Starting compensation
Scope of job responsibilities
Comfort with co-workers
Corporate culture
Location
Nature of job responsibilities
Challenges of the job
Opportunities for promotion
Commitment to continuous training/education
Utilizing my skills/developing new skills
Importance of job to the company
Job security
Travel (daily and/or overnight)
Size of employer
Commitment to community welfare
Products or services
Starting date
Work/life balance

Your own list, which may reflect other considerations, will be uniquely yours.

MISTAKE #89

"Accept" a job that hasn't been offered.

This is akin to counting your chickens before they have hatched. Some people assume that if an interview went well, or the interviewer says things that sound encouraging, they will be offered the job. That simply isn't so. The interviewer may think that you are a wonderful person, but not the best match for the job. Some employers feel compelled to make encouraging remarks to all candidates. Also, be aware that even an oral offer of employment (unless the job would be very short term) is not money in the bank.

Solution

Until you receive a job offer in writing, don't consider it official. If you have interviews scheduled with other companies, you should go through with them.

HINT: If you receive an oral offer, your initial response should be enthusiastic ("This is wonderful," "I am so happy," etc.), then ask when you might expect to receive a formal offer letter in the mail.

MISTAKE #90

Accept a job that pays well even though you will dislike it.

Some people will accept a job they know they just won't like to earn the kind of money that will buy them what they want for weekends and vacations. This is a matter of individual choice, but it is definitely a mistake if you find that you are trapped in an unhappy situation without options.

Solution

Remember that *having* more is not the same as *being* more. Having more money or possessions does not make you more happy, more popular, or more of a person. You are a total person, irrespective of how many cars, houses, etc you have. If you scale back your material desires, you will give yourself a great deal more flexibility to find a job that brings you more satisfaction. You may also find that, in doing so, you have more to share in terms of what is important with your spouse, children, and other significant people in your life. They in turn will also be happier.

MISTAKE #91

Accept an offer without taking another look at the employer.

Mike was thrilled when he received his offer from Happyco. "I am going to call them immediately and accept. This is a job that I will love and there is no point in delaying." Luckily his friend, Dan, suggested a somewhat calmer response: "It would be a good idea to visit Happyco one more time before responding."

Solution

Dan offered good advice. Here's why:

- **Visiting under less stressful conditions.** Mike would get a chance to see the work environment without being under the stress of a job interview. In this follow-up visit, he could experience the company's culture better and meet with people on a day that they weren't under the legal and professional strictures that are part of an interview situation.

- **Asking questions.** During the interview, Mike felt constrained about asking some questions. Also, some questions occurred to him after he returned home. At the follow-up visit, he can ask whatever he wants because he has the offer letter. (Of course, being less restrained doesn't mean he should be any less professional and polite.) The answers to Mike's questions may have an important influence on his decision to accept (or reject) the offer.

- **Clarifying the employer's expectations.** Perhaps Mike already asked his prospective manager, "What will be your performance expectations for me over the next year, the next three years?" If he has not asked about expectations, this may be his last chance to do so. After all, the job description is one thing, the manager's expectations may be another. Mike can also use the follow-up visit to meet again with the prospective manager and discuss matters requiring clarification.

- **Achieving peace of mind.** One of the worst things a person can do is to start a new job with nagging doubts. Therefore, let's assume that Michael learns absolutely nothing new from his follow-up visit. He has invested an additional day and reaped considerable peace of mind because he can now make his decision calmly and based on the best, most complete information available to him.

Many companies actually welcome a request for a follow-up visit. It is to their advantage that employees accept their job offer on a wholehearted and well-informed basis. To arrange a follow-up visit, call the person who signed your offer letter, express your joy and enthusiasm, then indicate something like this: "This is a very important decision and it would help me to see the place where I would be working one more time. Would it be possible for me to spend a day, or at least half a day, speaking with (name of manager) and some of my co-workers? Also, if possible, could I just take an unescorted walk around?" Some companies may even reimburse you for the reasonable expenses associated with your follow-up visit.

MISTAKE #92

Fail to negotiate compensation.

Michelle was underpaid for the work she did, simply because she hadn't asked for more at the time she was offered her job. Such a mistake may have a financial impact throughout her career.

Solution

You should negotiate a salary offer, being careful to take the right approach. For any given job, it is better to be paid more money than less money. Since in many jobs, bonuses and the following year's salary are based on your current salary, your starting salary often impacts your future salary as well. Even if you are unable to negotiate a higher salary, you will have peace of mind, avoiding the nagging doubt that you could have gotten more money if you had only tried. Nagging doubts are bad for your morale.

Here are some things to remember if salary negotiation makes you uncomfortable:

- **It is not pushy, rude, or impolite to seek an improved compensation package.** It is common sense, even expected, that a job candidate will negotiate a salary offer.

- **Ask for more when all other issues are resolved.** You should know in your heart that you want the job in terms of the work you would be doing, your comfort with the employer, the location, and the start date. If there are issues with those aspects, you should resolve them before money is discussed.

- **Asking face-to-face is best.** It is easier for people to say yes and harder to say no when a question is raised in person. Therefore, the best time for you to ask for more is at your follow-up visit, after you have received an offer.

- **Have solid reasons to back up your request.** You should be able to identify reasons why you are worth more to your employer than the initial offer might indicate. For example, you might cite salaries paid for a comparable position with other companies in the region or in the industry; skills you can bring with you above those which are helpful for the job even though they are not in the job description. However, you will not say that you expect more simply because you have two children to put through college (or any other kind of expenses that are important to you but not to the company's profitability).

- **Asking for more won't cost you your job offer if you ask in the right way.** Asking for anything, let alone money, can feel awkward, but imagine how you will feel if you don't ask, and subsequently find out that you could have gotten more! You can initiate the discussion by saying to your prospective manager something like this, albeit in your own words, "I love this job and everything about it. I love what I would be doing, the company, the location, and the color of the rugs. Most of all, I would look forward to working for you. There is only one thing that is making me hesitate and that is the starting salary. I was expecting something closer to $70,000 based on the scope of my responsibilities and the experience that I bring. If you could move the offer from $63,000 closer to $70,000, I would say yes right away." Stated this way, you have asked for more without falling into two pitfalls: 1) You did not make a counter offer. For example, you did not say, "I will accept this position only if you offer me $70,000." 2) You did not leave your manager wondering what you would say if the salary offer were indeed increased. Any fear that you might say "no" even to an increased offer would inhibit your manager from offering the increase in the first place.

- **Be prepared if the answer is "no."** You must remember that the discussion is about money, not love. If your manager does not increase the offer, this is not a negative reflection on your character or self-worth. Further, you must think about what your reaction will be, especially if your prospective boss says "no" right on the spot. Fortunately, if you have followed our advice, you have not painted yourself into a corner with your request. You can say something like, "I am disappointed about the response to my request for an increase in starting salary. If you had said yes, I would have said yes on the spot. But I understand that there are constraints on what you can do about salaries. I am still interested in this job and in this company. I will let you know soon if I can accept your offer. Would next week be timely enough for you?" By being prepared for a no, you will avoid most of the awkwardness of the situation, and feel better about yourself as well as the company.

MISTAKE #93

Accept an offer because of the people, not the job itself.

Would you marry or not marry someone based on how you feel about his or her cousin? Probably not. Unfortunately, Bill was on the verge of making an employment decision on that basis. He was about to say yes to a job offer because "Everybody has been so nice to me throughout the interview process. They really seem to want me and I would hate to disappoint them." Luckily, a friend gave Bill some good advice. "Bill, so far you have told me that people were very nice. But you haven't given any indication that you would like doing the job that was offered to you. You seem ready to make a major decision based on a factor that is nice but not central to the issue at hand."

Solution

Here are some questions to ask yourself as you consider whether to accept the job offer. Are the nice people whom you met the employees you would be working with, and do you know what they are like when they are not speaking with you as a job candidate? How did you feel about your prospective manager? Have you even spent a significant amount of time with him or her?

You should not worry about hurting someone's feelings if you turn down the offer. As long as you are polite about it, everyone will understand that you are making a professional decision.

MISTAKE #94

Fail to get everything in writing.

A job offer should be made in writing before you considerate it as official. But it would be a mistake to assume that something is part of the offer just because you discussed it orally.

Solution

A good offer letter clearly states the following:

- Title of the position

- Department of which the position is a part

- Salary (specified by payroll period; perhaps annualized) or wage (specified by hour)

- Probationary review terms and dates, if applicable

- Reference to first and subsequent annual reviews

- Date, time, and place to report

- Anything that you will need to bring with you on your first day of work

MISTAKE #95

Forget to thank everyone who helped you in your job search.

Courtesy never goes out of season. Thank all those who have helped you, including people with whom you spoke on an informational basis, your college alumni office, those in your network (old or new) whom you reached out to at any point in your job search process. You turned to them in your time of need. Don't forget them in your time of joy.

15

Making Mistakes in Special Circumstances

Some job seekers are prone to certain types of mistakes due to their special circumstances: transitioning military personnel, minorities, people with disabilities, and recent or forthcoming college graduates.

Those leaving military service face an often-difficult transition to the civilian world. Unfortunately, many of these veterans do not take advantage of the transition programs available to them or networking possibilities among one another. Further, military veterans often don't know how to address civilian misperceptions of military experience. If you have served in the military, you deserve the respect and gratitude of your countrymen. You also owe it to yourself to avoid the mistakes you will learn about in this chapter.

Members of minority groups are not the only people who make job search mistakes, but there are some mistakes that may require special attention. Among the pitfalls discussed in this chapter are making ethnicity an issue and assuming non-minority interviewers have a negative attitude.

Everyone has limitations of some sort, but each of us should market our *abilities*, not our disabilities. Some of the job-seeking mistakes made by people with disabilities are uncertainty about whether to disclose their disability, not addressing legitimate job-related issues, and misunderstanding the Americans with Disabilities Act.

Recent or forthcoming college graduates often make what sportscasters call "rookie mistakes." Mistakes common to them include trying to go it alone, confusing major with career, false expectations, and unprofessional job search conduct.

TRANSITIONING MILITARY

MISTAKE #1

Be unprepared for the transition to civilian life.

The transition from a military life to the civilian world can be difficult, and many veterans hurt themselves by not being adequately prepared for a job search in the civilian sector.

Solution

- **Take advantage of the military's transition programs while still in uniform.** By law, the various branches of the armed services must provide transition programs to those returning to civilian life. It is important to take advantage of these transition programs while you are still in the military because once you become a civilian, those programs are no longer available to you.

- **Be sure to utilize networking opportunities.** There are millions of military veterans in the US, and there are a number of self-help organizations that can be of great value to them. There is no need to go it alone. If you are or will be a veteran, here are some of the groups that you should be aware of:

American Legion
American Veterans (AMVETS)
Association for Service Disabled Veterans
Association of Military Surgeons of the United States
Blinded Veterans Association
Disabled American Veterans
Heli-Vets
Military Order of the Purple Heart
National Association of Uniformed Services
National Military Intelligence Association
Non-Commissioned Officers Association
Omega Delta Sigma
Paralyzed Veterans of America
Prisoner of War Net
Reserve Officers Association
The Retired Enlisted Association
The Retired Officers Association
The Retired Sergeants Major and Chiefs Association
Sigma Phi Psi
Veterans of Foreign Wars of the United States
Veterans of the Vietnam War
Vietnam Helicopter Flight Crew Network

Vietnam Helicopter Pilots Association
Vietnam Veterans of America
Women Officers Professional Association

MISTAKE #2

Fail to understand civilian misperceptions about military experience.

Theresa Arndt, Coordinator, Veterans Employment Programs for the state of Oregon, has some solid ideas about common civilian misperceptions and how you can handle them successfully:

Solution

MISCONCEPTION: The military discourages people from thinking independently. They just follow orders.

REALITY: Enlisted personnel and officers alike are trained to act in a leadership capacity for a platoon or squadron of men and women. Many have college educations and have taken special courses in leadership. They understand the concept of team and all work toward a common goal. They are not rattled by the unexpected. They are trained to operate under very adverse and critical conditions. They can think on their feet in a crisis situation and can work in extremely tight time frames when needed (and without much complaint). Since veterans have been trained to look for ways of doing things more effectively, they could thus help their civilian employers improve the quality of their products or services.

MISCONCEPTION: Officers don't have a work ethic. They just give orders.

REALITY: Officers also take orders from superior officers and are tasked with seeing that subordinates realize the intent of their orders. Officers must be either college graduates or are commissioned in wartime as recognized leaders. Some officers have earned graduate degrees. They are held accountable for the efforts of large groups of servicemen and women and must understand the mission and the processes of the staff they oversee. Most now do the work alongside their enlisted members and are trained in mission-critical preparedness.

MISCONCEPTION: Veterans cannot relate to non-veteran civilians.

REALITY: Veterans learn to get along with many different cultures, ethnicities, and personal differences. Most military veterans make friends fairly easily and quickly, being accustomed to living among various cultures worldwide throughout their career. They thus have a support system or "family" of sorts wherever they are stationed.

MISCONCEPTION: Vets won't be able to relate to a manager who may be younger.

REALITY: Some of the most senior military members have officers above them who are younger than they are. This is not a new phenomenon to the military. The real crux of the issue is that, whether they are enlisted or officers, military people are taught to follow the orders of whoever is in command. To fail in this would be a dereliction of duty and punishable by the military judicial system. A lot more stringent than in civilian life, wouldn't you say?

MISCONCEPTION: The military is not a business, therefore ex-military personnel don't understand profit/loss considerations.

REALITY: People in the military are there to make sure the business of our armed services runs smoothly as possible. Supplies and product are critical and they make the best use of them. The mission of business is to get the product produced at the highest quality to the customer at the lowest production cost, a mission that military veterans would understand.

MISTAKE #3

Use military terminology in your resume.

Civilian employers frequently fail to understand military terms and acronyms used in resumes. Thus, such resumes might be passed over in favor of others having more understandable language.

Solution

Make sure your resume and cover letter contain civilian terminology. Selma had been a disbursement officer in the Navy, and was having trouble getting an interview. She found out incidentally at a party that civilians didn't understand what her job had been. As is the case with many vets, Selma simply assumed that everyone would understand what she did. After all, that had been the case in the service. She resolved the problem by utilizing the terminology converter found at Vetjobs.com. There she learned that her military experience was cognate to the civilian experience of working with payrolls and banks. Once her resume started to speak in civilian language, she began getting invited to interviews.

MISTAKE #4

Overlook certifications earned during military service.

Ted made a mistake similar to Selma's. In his case, he forgot to state explicitly on his resume that he had achieved a number of certifications in computer programs.

Since his military occupation specialty would have required those certifications, Ted just assumed that everyone would know that he had them. Similarly, Tom missed out on a strong selling point by not citing on his resume the MBA -level management courses he had taken through the Army, because he assumed civilian employers would know that those courses were part of his staff officer training.

Solution

Don't assume civilian employers are fully aware of certifications you earned or courses you took during your military career. Put them on your resume to show the knowledge and skills you have acquired.

MISTAKE #5

Expect civilians to give you preferential treatment because of your rank.

Arnold was justly proud of his service to his country and that he had achieved the rank of major prior to leaving the military. Unfortunately, even in his civilian attire, he expected people to be aware of his military rank and show him special respect because of it. That attitude was transmitted during civilian job interviews with consistently negative results.

Solution

Be careful about wearing your rank on your sleeve. Organizations are reluctant to hire people who expect deference based on military rank, because deference in the private sector is based on track record within the company or organization, not on achievements elsewhere. Arnold had to learn to distinguish between the characteristics that helped him become a major (leadership, organization, dedication to task), and the significance of the rank itself.

MISTAKE #6

Give military-style answers in interviews.

Leon didn't understand that civilians tend to like fairly concise answers, even to open-ended questions. When he was asked, "Tell me about yourself," he started with his ROTC experience and discussed each of his subsequent military duty experiences. It would have been better to give a concise answer and wait for the interviewers to ask a follow-up question to become more expansive. There is a good drill on VetJobs.com in this regard, reproduced below with the author's permission.

HOW TO CREATE AN ORAL RESUME—
"The Two Minute Drill"

When you are asked "Tell me about yourself," here's how to respond. You should be able to cover all this within two minutes.

1. Name, Professional Designation, and Career Objective

   My name is ...
   I am a ...
   I am seeking ...

2. Professional Background and Current Situation (if appropriate)

   I have ____ years experience as...
   My positions/assignments include ...

3. Education, Training, and Professional Preparation

   My education and training have prepared me for ...
   I have ....

4. Career Highlights and Recent Accomplishments

   In my work as a _____, I have ...
   Most recently, I have...

5. Relevance to the Potential Employer

   I firmly believe my skills and experience could benefit you (or a_____ company) in the following ways:

6. Positive Closing

   I am eager to ...

MINORITIES

Are there some mistakes that members of minority groups should be especially careful to avoid? Nobody has a monopoly on mistakes, but here are a few that African Americans, Hispanic Americans, and Native Americans might watch out for. Based on her years of experience as a human resources professional, Lorraine Mixon-Page, Senior Professional in Human Resources (SPHR), who has chaired the Society for Human Resource Management (SHRM) Workplace Diversity Committee, calls attention to these potential mistakes.

MISTAKE #1

Fail to do your research.

Isn't doing your research and being prepared for the interview necessary for *any* job seeker? Of course it is. However, there are two reasons why your research is especially important if you are a member of a minority group. First, it is unfortunately true that a minority applicant may need to go just "a little further" than other applicants in pursuing jobs, especially in a tight job market. Second, by doing your research and being prepared, you are making it clear that you don't expect to get the job "just because you are minority."

Solution

Learn as much as you can about the company or organization, through checking its website, SEC documents, business media, websites pertaining to its line of business or service, and your local public library. If you are sending a hardcopy cover letter, know the name and title of the specific person to whom it should be addressed. That might be the person in charge of human resources or the hiring manager for a specific position. If you are invited to an interview, make sure that you are knowledgeable about the company and can articulate how your skills and knowledge can benefit the company, as well as why you want that specific job. Make a list of good questions of your own to ask.

MISTAKE #2

Emphasize your race or ethnic heritage on your resume.

Your race or ethnic heritage should always be a fact that you are proud of, but never a *factor* on your resume.

Solution

Be proud of your heritage—for example, Black. But listing *only* Black fraternities/sororities, professional associations, and/or civic groups on your resume may give the impression that you want to be interviewed simply for being Black rather than for your talents, or that you are comfortable only with that ethnic group. When you list those organizations, ask yourself, "What is my purpose in including this on my resume?" If the answer is that you want to show leadership, community involvement, or professional recognition, that's fine. If you are only trying to say that you are Black, reconsider.

As is the case with all job applicants, you should *never* include a photograph of yourself with your resume.

MISTAKE #3

Make the ethnicity of the interviewer an issue.

Some people assume that if the interviewer is a Caucasian or an Anglo, that person is biased against minority candidates—an inaccurate assumption in most cases. If you harbor a negative assumption about the interviewer, it will impact adversely on your effectiveness during the interview.

Solution

It is in your best interests to assume that the interviewer is a fair-minded person, as is usually the case. Conversely, if the interviewer is Black, Hispanic, or Native American, do not assume that you have found a kinsman who is going to favor you. Most interviewers will be concerned if you seem to be relating to them based on ethnic affinity instead of on your qualifications for the job or your interest in their company.

MISTAKE #4

Assume that "not used to" means "prejudiced."

There may be some people whom you meet during the interview process who seem a bit uncomfortable in your presence.

Solution

It is possible that they are simply not used to being in the company of people from your ethnic group. That is a far cry from holding a prejudice. Besides, some people are simply uncomfortable with strangers—any strangers. Assuming the worst about others will not help bring out the best in you.

MISTAKE #5

Ask "lawsuit" questions.

As with all job applicants, you will probably be asked if you have any questions for the interviewer. If you ask racially based questions in the wrong way, you will harm your chances of a job offer.

Solution

If you want to ask questions of a racial nature, be sure of two things:

1. Ask in the right way. For example, if you are interested in the company's affirmative action plan, you could say, "I read on your website that you have an affirmative action plan. That is a good thing to have, but it can be difficult to carry out sometimes, even with the best of intentions. Do you feel that your affirmative action policy is working out well?" On the other hand, saying, "Tell me about your affirmative action plan" may put the interviewer on the defensive. Asking, "What is wrong with you people? I don't see many minorities around here" would be offensive to almost anyone.

2. Don't make race the only topic of your questions. You are not a Johnny-one-note (I hope), so don't give people the wrong impression.

MISTAKE #6

Keep your job search "minority-specific."

You limit your job opportunities by checking only those job boards associated with your ethnic group, or attending only minority-targeted job fairs.

Solution

There is a big world out there. Take advantage of all of it.

PEOPLE WITH DISABILITIES

All job seekers, with or without disabilities, have limitations, and everyone should be proud of what they can do. Whatever your disability, market your abilities. The job application and interview process should focus on your job qualifications, not on your disability. The Human Factors Consultants at the Job Accommodation Network (a service of the Office of Disability Policy of the U.S. Department of Labor) know from years of experience that people with all types of functional limitations and disabilities can enhance their success as job seekers handling their disability the right way.

MISTAKE #1

Believe that you are obligated to disclose your disability.

Some people believe that honesty at a job interview requires revealing information about their disability. As with all job interviews, you must be truthful in what you say, but you don't have to volunteer information that is not relevant to the performance of the job.

Solution

Do not raise the issue of a disability until you know that it is going to be a factor in doing the job. Keep in mind that information about your disability may not be relevant during the job-seeking process. There are, however, at least two exceptions.

First, if your disability will be a factor at the interview, let the employer know that fact when you arrange the time and place for the interview. For example, if you are deaf and would be more comfortable using an interpreter, let the employer know ahead of time that you will need the services of an interpreter at the interview.

Second, if your disability will be a competitive advantage, you should disclose it early on, perhaps in your cover letter. Although this is a relatively uncommon occurrence, there are several possible scenarios for this. Judy is applying for a job with a state or federal agency that must comply with affirmative action policies. Alan is applying for a job that directly relates to his experience as a person with a disability, such as a rehabilitation counselor. Harry is applying for a position where having a disability is a qualification for the position—for example, a job as a substance abuse counselor may require that an applicant be a recovering alcoholic.

MISTAKE #2

Not know in advance possible barriers you may face.

People with disabilities must anticipate what barriers they might be confronted with during the interview process and in their doing the job effectively. For example, if you are a wheelchair user, you should get acquainted with the building where your interview will take place. Are there are physical barriers to your entrance and movement? If you are hearing impaired, what will you need to handle the interview effectively and what accommodations might you need to perform the essential functions of the job?

Solution

Once you have arranged an interview, a call to the human resources office should result in answers to your questions. Delve into the job description. Are there aspects of the job that would require some sort of accommodation for you? Once you have anticipated the barriers you will face, you can let the employer know how you will perform the job effectively.

MISTAKE #3

Fail to use available resources in your job search.

People with disabilities who fail to check out and take advantage of the array of resources that can help them find jobs limit their employment opportunities.

Solution

There are many vocational rehabilitation and social service agencies that can assist you in your job search. A gateway website to state vocational and rehabilitation agencies is http://trfn.clpgh.org/srac/state-vr.html.

There are also many private and nonprofit disability-related employment resources operated by commercial enterprises. A good source of information is the Job Accommodation Network website, http://www.jan.wvu.edu.

MISTAKE #4

Confuse ignorance with hostility.

Your interviewer may be uncomfortable around people with disabilities. Do not confuse discomfort with hostility.

Solution

Many people, including your future co-workers, may be uncomfortable around people with disabilities, but well intentioned. Being prepared to sensitize your interviewers and future co-workers is a constructive step. Assuming the worst about them is not.

MISTAKE #5

Misunderstand the limitations of the ADA.

Some people with disabilities assume the Americans With Disabilities Act guarantees them a job regardless of qualifications.

Solution

Everyone on earth faces at least one reality in common: there are some jobs that we simply are not capable of doing. For example, a person who is blind cannot be a pilot, and a person with a bad back cannot lift 100-pound bags of cement all day. While you should feel free to apply for any job of interest to you, it is also important to understand that the Americans with Disabilities Act (ADA) does not consider it discriminatory to turn down a job applicant who cannot perform the essential functions of the job. The ADA does not guarantee jobs for people with disabilities. The law merely states that if a candidate with a disability is equally qualified to perform the essential functions of the job, s/he is entitled to equal consideration for the job. It does not say the employer has to hire that person.

RECENT OR UPCOMING COLLEGE GRADUATES

Dr. Robert Greenberg, Assistant Vice Provost for Student Affairs and Director of Career Services at the University of Tennessee (Knoxville), has identified 11 job-seeking mistakes that are especially common among upcoming or recent college graduates. All of these mistakes can be avoided if you become aware of them and adjust your attitude where necessary.

MISTAKE #1

Try to search for a job on your own.

Many students decide that they are going to find a job on their own, not realizing how much going "solo" limits their access to the vast work world out there.

Solution

A crucial part of the job search process is networking with others, including family and friends, other students, professors, and former employers and co-workers. People who advance successfully in their careers know how to seek advice and counsel from the networks they developed throughout the years. Students or recent grads may not yet have developed enough confidence to feel comfortable asking for help. The irony is that those who are asked for help are usually more than happy to provide it. Someday, you may be able to return the favor.

MISTAKE #2

Accept advice unquestioningly.

The flip side of going it alone is to blindly accept whatever advice (perhaps unsolicited) that you get. Young people tend to listen to their peers, who may not be knowledgeable. They may have formed a strong opinion about a company based on how "cool" their product or a favorite TV program. Parents, family friends, and faculty may also offer advice, however well-meaning.

Solution

Remember that people have their own perspectives, which may not conform to your value system or even be accurate or appropriate. Ask, listen, probe politely, do your research, and then evaluate.

MISTAKE #3

Handcuff yourself to your major.

Many students mistakenly think that their major has determined their career. Lou might say, "My major was advertising so I suppose I should go into advertising." Andrea might say, "I am an English major. What can I do with that?"

Solution

Your major doesn't guarantee you anything, and it doesn't put any career handcuffs on you, either. Think in terms of what you would like to do in your career and go forward from there.

MISTAKE #4

Have false expectations.

Yes you are bright and have lots of potential. However, if you have inflated expectations, an employer is much less likely to hire you. Among typical false expectations are high salary/bonus, nice title, private office, glamorous responsibilities, rapid advancement, business trips to interesting places, and frequent vacations. Employers know that people with these expectations tend to become disgruntled, underperform and then quit.

Solution

Make sure that you are fully aware of the reality of entry-level positions taken by college graduates. Talk to as many people as you can about the nature of their jobs, especially at the entry-level stage. Especially seek out those who are employed in the field you want to enter.

MISTAKE #5

Rely on a single source of job leads.

Many students seem content to use just the Internet to post a few resumes and respond to a few job board notices. The computer can be very seductive. As a student you are an expert in using it and you can always tell yourself (and your parents) that you actively are looking for a job with a few clicks of your mouse. It is also relatively impersonal so you may feel that you are not putting yourself on the line. The computer (and by extension the Internet) is a tool, not a complete solution.

Solution

A successful search usually requires using a variety of sources, including your campus career services office, the faculty, networking, professional association directories, and the Internet. Besides, finding a job is more about contact with people than merely using technology.

MISTAKE #6

Exhibit a lack of direction.

The key word here is "exhibiting." It is likely that you don't have a clear and definite sense of direction at this stage in your life. The problem is, if you reveal a lack of direction in your job search, you are likely to be perceived as *totally undirected* and/or likely to take any job that comes along.

Solution

On your resume, have an objective or summary that indicates, at least broadly, what type of job you are seeking. For example,"seeking a position in finance" or " pursuing a career that utilizes my writing and creative abilities." At a job interview, you will likely be asked, "Why do you want to work for us?" Notice the question does not end in the word "only." Treat this as a concrete question dealing with the foreseeable future, rather than a theoretical question dealing with the next 40 years. Tell the interviewer what it you like about the job and the company as well. The fact that you are not absolutely certain about your career plans does not have to enter the discussion.

MISTAKE #7

Confuse "inappropriate" with "candid."

During job interviews some students discuss their weaknesses instead of their strengths. Others may bring up their personal life (as in parties, drinking, and romantic problems) instead of professionally relevant issues. They think that by doing so they are being candid with the interviewer. In reality they are showing a lack of understanding of what is appropriate to discuss during job interviews.

Solution

Employers are hiring your *professional* self, not your private self, and the professional self is what should be presented to them, rather than discussing personal matters. Keep personal issues to yourself.

MISTAKE #8

"I hide it; you find it."

You may be uncomfortable talking about your virtues and strengths. Unfortunately, many students deal with this discomfort by deciding that they should not sell themselves and that it is the interviewer's responsibility to discern their positives.

Solution

A good guideline is this: If you don't say it, the interviewer won't hear it. Your responsibility is to make your strengths shine forth in your answers and questions you ask at your job interview.

MISTAKE #9

Keep sloppy records.

Dennis had a good initial interview on campus and was invited to a follow-up interview on site at the company. There, he was asked to name his initial interviewer. Dennis couldn't remember the person's name because he had not taken note of it.

Solution

You should make notes after every interview, including the name of your interviewer. Otherwise you look like the fifth grader who tells the teacher that the dog ate his homework.

MISTAKE #10

Use sloppy language.

Janice forgot that she was at a job interview and spoke as though she were chatting with her friends in the dorm.

Solution

You should avoid using slang or college lingo. Interjections such as "you know" and "like" will hurt your chances. For example, instead of "cool, " say "interesting."

MISTAKE #11

Criticize a former employer.

Kim told her interviewer that her job at a local fast food shop was "stupid" and that the manager was a "jerk." Badmouthing a former employer is often fatal to your future employment opportunities. David made a similar mistake when he blamed his professors for some less than stellar grades.

Solution

No one demands perfection, but everybody will expect you to take responsibility for your own actions and to learn from your mistakes. Tearing down others does nothing to build yourself up. *Never* do this during a job interview.

Index

Author Biography

Richard Fein is a nationally recognized expert in career and job search issues. He has been a contributor to the *Wall Street Journal's* "Managing Your Career" and a columnist for *Employment Review Magazine*. His books have been reviewed by syndicated columnists Joyce Lain Kennedy, Diane Lewis, and Paula Ancona. Richard has also been a frequent commentator on the job search process for both print and electronic media. He has appeared as a guest on more than 30 radio and television programs and has been quoted in newspapers as diverse as the *Christian Science Monitor* and the *Idaho Statesman*.

Richard holds an MBA from Baruch College in New York, an MA in Political Science from the City University of New York, and a BA in Political Science from the University of Pennsylvania. He is currently the Director of Undergraduate Placement Services at the Isenberg School of Management, University of Massachusetts in Amherst.

Available for interviews and consultation, Richard can be contacted through the publisher.

Career Resources

The following Career Resources are available directly from Impact Publications. Full descriptions of each title as well as nine downloadable catalogs, videos, and software can be found on our website: www.impactpublications.com. Complete the following form or list the titles, include shipping (see formula at the end), enclose payment, and send your order to:

IMPACT PUBLICATIONS
9104 Manassas Drive, Suite N
Manassas Park, VA 20111-5211 USA
1-800-361-1055 (orders only)
Tel. 703-361-7300 or Fax 703-335-9486
Email address: info@impactpublications.com
Quick & easy online ordering: www.impactpublications.com

Orders from individuals must be prepaid by check, money order, or major credit card. We accept telephone, fax, and email orders.

Qty.	TITLES	Price	TOTAL
Featured Title			
_____	**95 Mistakes Job Seekers Make**	$13.95	_____
College-to-Career Resources			
_____	200 Best Jobs for College Graduates	16.95	_____
_____	America's Top Jobs for College Graduates	15.95	_____
_____	Best Resumes for College Students and New Grads	12.95	_____
_____	College Majors Handbook	24.95	_____
_____	Great Careers in Two Years	19.95	_____
_____	The Job Hunting Guide	14.95	_____
_____	Quick Guide to College Majors and Careers	16.95	_____
Testing and Assessment			
_____	Career Tests	12.95	_____
_____	Discover the Best Jobs for You	15.95	_____
_____	Discover What You're Best At	14.00	_____
_____	Do What You Are	18.95	_____
_____	What Type Am I?	14.95	_____

Inspiration and Empowerment

_____ Life Strategies	13.95	_____
_____ Maximum Success	24.95	_____
_____ Seven Habits of Highly Effective People	14.00	_____
_____ Who Moved My Cheese?	19.95	_____

Career Exploration and Job Strategies

_____ 50 Cutting Edge Jobs	15.95	_____
_____ 95 Mistakes Job Seekers Make	13.95	_____
_____ 100 Great Jobs and How to Get Them	17.95	_____
_____ Best Jobs for the 21st Century	19.95	_____
_____ Best Keywords for Resumes, Cover Letters, Interviews	17.95	_____
_____ Change Your Job, Change Your Life (8th Edition)	17.95	_____
_____ Internships	26.95	_____
_____ No One Will Hire Me!	13.95	_____
_____ Occupational Outlook Handbook	16.95	_____
_____ What Color Is Your Parachute?	17.95	_____

Internet Job Search

_____ America's Top Internet Job Sites	19.95	_____
_____ CareerXroads (annual)	26.95	_____
_____ e-Resumes	11.95	_____
_____ Haldane's Best Employment Websites for Professionals	15.95	_____

Resumes and Letters

_____ 201 Dynamite Job Search Letters	19.95	_____
_____ Cover Letters for Dummies	16.99	_____
_____ Haldane's Best Cover Letters for Professionals	15.95	_____
_____ Haldane's Best Resumes for Professionals	15.95	_____
_____ High Impact Resumes and Letters (8th Edition)	19.95	_____
_____ Resumes for Dummies	16.99	_____
_____ The Savvy Resume Writer	12.95	_____

Networking

_____ A Foot in the Door	14.95	_____
_____ How to Work a Room	14.00	_____
_____ Masters of Networking	16.95	_____
_____ The Savvy Networker	13.95	_____

Dress, Image, and Etiquette

_____ Dressing Smart for Men	14.95	_____
_____ Dressing Smart for Women	14.95	_____

Interviews and Salary Negotiations

_____ 101 Dynamite Questions to Ask At Your Job Interview	13.95	_____
_____ Dynamite Salary Negotiations	15.95	_____
_____ Haldane's Best Answers to Tough Interview Questions	15.95	_____
_____ Haldane's Best Salary Tips for Professionals	15.95	_____
_____ Interview for Success (8th Edition)	15.95	_____

_____	Job Interviews for Dummies	16.99	_____
_____	Nail the Job Interview!	13.95	_____
_____	The Savvy Interviewer	10.95	_____

SUBTOTAL _____

Virginia residents add 4½% sales tax _____

POSTAGE/HANDLING ($5 for first product and 8% of SUBTOTAL) _____

8% of SUBTOTAL $5.00

TOTAL ENCLOSED _____

SHIP TO:

NAME _____

ADDRESS _____

_____

_____

PAYMENT METHOD:

❑ I enclose check/money order for $ _____ made payable to IMPACT PUBLICATIONS.

❑ Please charge $ _____ to my credit card:

❑ Visa   ❑ MasterCard   ❑ American Express   ❑ Discover

Card # _____ Expiration date: ___/___/

Signature _____

Keep in Touch . . .
On the Web!

www.impactpublications.com
www.ishoparoundtheworld.com
www.hoteltravelshop.com
www.mycruiseshop.com
www.contentfortravel.com
www.winningthejob.com
www.veteransworld.com
www.contentforcareers.com